MW01004144

MURDER AT
BREAKHEART HILL FARM

The Shocking 1900 Case that
Gripped Boston's North Shore

DOUGLAS L. HEATH
AND ALISON C. SIMCOX

THE
History
PRESS

Published by The History Press
Charleston, SC
www.historypress.com

First published 2020

Manufactured in the United States

ISBN 9781467143691

Library of Congress Control Number: 2020938619

To our sons, Ian and Alec

CONTENTS

PREFACE

We came across the story of the murder of George E. Bailey while writing our book *Breakheart Reservation*. That book chronicles the transformation of a six-hundred-acre parcel of colonial common land, now mostly in Saugus, Massachusetts, into a private hunting retreat and, ultimately, into one of the most popular parks in the state park system. While doing research for *Breakheart Reservation*, we often took hikes there and stopped at the rustic visitor center to warm ourselves in front of the fireplace. Imagine our surprise when our research revealed that a horrific murder had occurred just a stone's throw away, and that the chief prosecutor in the murder trial was Hosea Knowlton, the famous prosecutor in the 1893 Lizzie Borden trial.

When we gave talks on *Breakheart Reservation*, we tried to focus on its broader history, but audiences invariably wanted to talk about the murder. We had some details, but clearly, there was more to the story. So, we went back into archives, court documents and old newspapers to fill in the missing pieces. As the mountain of research grew, we realized that we had a book waiting to be written, with a cast of characters right out of the pages of Dickens, including paupers, neglected children, muddleheaded drunkards, greedy villains and scenes stretching from New Brunswick to Boston.

The year was 1900 and the place was Breakheart Hill farm. At that time, more than half of the nation's population lived on similar farms. Farmers produced crops for their families and for local sale and made or traded nearly everything they needed. Perhaps because of this self-sufficiency and the belief that life was simpler, family farms have been romanticized, but at Breakheart Hill farm, something went terribly wrong.

George Bailey, the caretaker of the farm, disappeared in October 1900. Some suspected that his farmhand, John Best, a coarse man who liked to drink, had played a role, but no one knew for sure. So began the story that dominated the Boston press for months and prompted thousands of people to descend on the Breakheart farm and, later, the Salem courthouse.

Key to telling this fascinating story were the online transcript of the criminal trial and microfilm of old newspapers preserved in libraries. We read over eight hundred pages of court transcript, sometimes with magnifying glass in hand, and reams of small, often faded print in the then eight Boston dailies, as well as the Lynn, Salem and Wakefield newspapers. These sources allowed us to tell the story using the actual words of the people involved, including the accused murderer and his sister, the victim and his "wife" Susie, the police and investigators and the owners of Breakheart Hill farm. The many newspaper illustrations of the crime scene and courtrooms drawn by talented artists provided pictures worth thousands of words, and through the marvel of the internet, we found and spoke with a descendant of Bailey, Mary Lou Bailey, who shared her knowledge of her family's history.

Ultimately, only George Bailey and his murderer knew what really happened. We present the evidence that was available to the jury, but we leave it to you to decide whether justice was served.

ACKNOWLEDGEMENTS

This book would not have been possible without access to the report of the capital case of the *Commonwealth of Massachusetts v. John C. Best*. In April 1903, Attorney General Herbert Parker got permission from Governor John Bates to publish the complete trial transcript because Parker believed that "the nature of the case, the line of evidence upon which it was prosecuted, and the issues of fact and law involved make it, to my mind, a case that will be remarkably instructive to the profession and interesting as a matter of judicial history." Added to this valuable record were regional newspapers that are archived online and on microfilm. The newspaper accounts were written in vivid detail and provided insights into the lives of the many people whose lives were touched by this horrific crime.

We thank our good friend Sally Rege Carroll and our son Ian for reading the manuscript and providing suggestions. This is a better book than it would have been without their contributions. Erin Falcone also provided excellent comments.

We are grateful to Brian Perry, Judith Loubris McCarthy and Mary Lou Bailey, who contributed photographs of Annie and Charles Deary, the gate to Breakheart Hill forest and the Bailey family. We also thank Karen Faler, who shared her husband Paul Faler's book on the Industrial Revolution in Lynn, Massachusetts.

The following organizations gave us access to newspaper microfilms and other materials: Beebe Memorial Library, Beverly Public Library, Boston Public Library, Lynn Public Library, Lynn Museum & Historical Society,

Acknowledgements

Lincoln County Historical Association (Wiscasset, Maine), Salem Public Library, Social Law Library, Middlesex South Registry of Deeds and Massachusetts Department of Conservation and Recreation. Last but not least, we thank our editors at The History Press, Michael Kinsella and Hayley Behal, who were supportive throughout.

1
THE VICTIM

George Bailey

Early Life

George Edward Bailey was born on June 18, 1859, in Alna, a farming community in southeast Maine along the Sheepscot River. He was the second of nine children born to Charles Bailey, a farmer and mail carrier, and Harriet Bailey, née Palmer. At that time, the river was a principal means of transportation and powered saw- and gristmills. Forests provided timber for houses and shipbuilding.

Completed ships were floated six miles south to Wiscasset, the deepest harbor north of Boston. In 1797, men floated the original masts for the USS *Constitution* "Old Ironsides" from Puddle Dock in Alna to Wiscasset, where they were towed to Boston. During the 1800s, Alna shipyards produced over one hundred schooners, brigs and other vessels. Even though Alna was known for shipbuilding, most people, like George Bailey's father, were farmers or were employed by tanneries, taverns, stores and other small businesses.[1]

Between 1856 and 1875, Charles and Harriet Bailey had a child about every two years. Unlike families who lost many children, all nine of theirs survived into adulthood. In 1870, Rachel (thirteen), George (ten), Jefferson (eight) and Henry (five) were attending a one-room schoolhouse in Alna. Another sister and brother were still at home. The following year, fourteen-year-old Rachel discovered she was pregnant and left school. In August, she married a local farmer, and in November, their first child was born.

Although people now assume that children go to school, this was not a given at that time. In Maine, attendance was not required until 1875 and only for those aged nine to fifteen for twelve weeks of the year. As well as going to school, the Bailey children, like other farm children, helped around the house and farm. Among their chores were scrubbing floors, churning butter, weeding the household garden, gathering eggs and firewood, hauling water, picking apples, feeding chickens and pigs and other farm animals and mucking out stalls.

George Bailey sat for this portrait at the F.F. Nadeau photography studio in Newmarket, New Hampshire, in about 1885. *Mary Lou Bailey.*

Most of the Bailey children settled in Alna and led useful, but unremarkable, lives. But George was different. From a young age, he acquired a reputation as a person to avoid. He grew to be a large and strong man, and few people dared to quarrel with him. Most left him alone. His brother Henry acknowledged that George was irritable but claimed that he had a kindly disposition and admired his willingness to try his hand at anything.

In about 1876, restless for adventure, George Bailey went to sea. In an interview with the *Lynn Daily Evening Item*, one of his brothers gave this account of his time at sea: "When George was about 17 years old, he began a seafaring life, and continued it for about three years, being in the West India trade. On his first voyage, he was second mate of the vessel, and the captain had a sort of mutiny on board. On the second trip of the barque, which was the style of the ship he sailed on, he was promoted to first mate, and finally became captain."[2]

He was a captain for only a short time before moving to the city of Lynn, about ten miles north of Boston, where he had heard that jobs were plentiful. In Lynn, George Bailey met Henry Mitchell, who had a pig farm in the neighboring town of Saugus. The two men got along well, and Mitchell offered Bailey a job on his farm and a temporary place to stay. In Saugus, Bailey found a town that was similar to his hometown of Alna. Although more industrial, with shoemaking, textile and tobacco industries, Saugus, like Alna, was a forested farming and mill community near the sea. It also had a river that flowed through town, the Saugus River, which powered gristmills and sawmills.[3]

Bailey soon found a better-paying job in nearby Wakefield delivering ice from Lake Quannapowitt to local residences, hotels and restaurants for the J.H. Cartland Ice Company. He moved from Saugus to a room in Wakefield but continued to travel to Saugus to help Mitchell on his farm. During the winter in Wakefield, Bailey mostly kept to himself but left a good impression with the local people. Years later, in a 1900 *Wakefield Daily Item* article, Bailey was characterized as having been a "genial, kindly man" whom everyone liked.[4]

During his free time, Bailey enjoyed the harness races at the Old Saugus Racetrack. He also liked to travel to Lynn, just a few stops away on the Saugus branch of the Eastern Railroad. At that time, 1882, Lynn was an industrial city with thriving shoemaking and leather industries and easy access to Boston via the steam-powered Eastern Railroad and Lynn Harbor. Barges continually arrived in the shallow harbor, bringing coal, lumber and animal hides.

Before 1850, shoes in Lynn were produced using a putting-out system in which families of shoemakers (or cordwainers) worked in small shops called ten-footers, located near their homes. Women worked as binders, sewing the shoe uppers, and men made the soles and attached the uppers to the soles. Merchants supplied families with materials and sold the finished product.

After 1850, machines, starting with the McKay Stitcher sewing machine, began replacing handwork, and the work moved from the home and workshops into factories. Lynn soon gained prominence for its production of ladies' fine shoes made of Morocco leather.[5] The shoe, leather and other factories drew immigrants by the thousands, mainly from England, Ireland and Canada, as well as workers from rural New England.

On his trips to Lynn, Bailey would step off an Eastern Railroad train at the station house in central Lynn onto dusty streets bustling with life and lined with brick factory buildings and blocks of shops selling dry goods, groceries, fish and meat, carriages, shoes, paints and thousands of other products. Men wearing worn wool suits, and many with bowler hats, and women in long dresses with high collars would be walking or standing in groups along sidewalks recently made from Portland cement.

Horse-drawn carriages, democrat wagons (light, flatbed, horse-drawn farm wagons) and buckboards would roll by, leaving clouds of dust in their wake. Bailey would pass tin-ware, leather goods, tobacco and other stores, keeping an eye out for pretty girls. Soon, he would head to one of the city's ninety-odd saloons, where men gathered to drink, gamble and chew tobacco.

These saloons commonly had a frontier atmosphere, with sawdust on the floor, spittoons in the corner and frequent fights. One of the most popular saloons was James Hennessey's in the basement of the old 1803 Lynn Hotel on Western Avenue. Bailey would stop there or at another saloon, such as the Crawford House on Andrew Street, Charles E. Jepson's on Union Street or George E. Russell's on Oxford Street, and order his favorite drink, cherry rum.[6]

Bailey was undoubtedly among the crowds in Lynn when P.T. Barnum's Greatest Show on Earth came to town on July 22, 1882. The entire city turned out to watch the caravan of ten elephants in the street parade, including the giant African elephant Jumbo, which had recently been bought from the London Zoo, and a baby elephant. Some twenty-five thousand people attended the show, which featured equestrian, acrobatic and other circus performances. It was the grandest and most costly show ever seen in Lynn. It was here that twenty-three-year-old Bailey most likely met fourteen-year-old Mary McNutt, a housekeeper.[7]

As Bailey's brother Benjamin later recounted, Mary was very pretty, and he was interested in her right away. Mary would have found it hard to resist a man like George Bailey, who was ruggedly handsome, strong and hardworking but also offered a potential way out of her life of abuse, poverty and servitude. The following year, in September 1883, they were married in the Central Congregational Church in Lynn. Even at that time, fourteen was an exceptionally young age to get married, so Mary told the clergyman that she was sixteen years old. Within two months, she was pregnant.[8]

Mary McNutt

Jacob McNutt, Mary's father, was born in 1834 in Truro, Nova Scotia. Like his father before him, he became a farmer. But in 1856, Jacob decided to join others who were moving from Canada's Maritime provinces to New England cities in search of jobs and a better life. He chose the growing city of Lynn and found work as a blacksmith by promoting skills he had acquired by working on a farm.

Jacob soon met a local girl, nineteen-year-old Sarah Bell, the daughter of a blacksmith. When she became pregnant, they did what many in their situation did and, in October 1856, got married. They moved to Market Street in the city center, and by 1872, they had moved six times and had nine children, only five of whom survived their first year.[9]

Amity Street in Lynn at the intersection with Washington Street (*foreground*). In 1869, Mary McNutt, Bailey's first wife, was born at 30 Amity Street. *Lynn Public Library.*

In 1869, the year that Mary was born, fire destroyed much of Lynn's central business district. The gutted buildings were replaced by five- and six-story factories. As the number of factories increased, so did the population.[10] From 1800 to 1850, when Lynn was incorporated as a city, the population had grown from three thousand to over fourteen thousand. By 1869, the city had over twenty-eight thousand people.[11]

As a blacksmith, Jacob McNutt had always been able to find work. However, the demand for blacksmiths declined as wrought iron and steel products, such as tools and nails, were increasingly made in factories. Like other tradesmen in Lynn and elsewhere, blacksmiths like McNutt were not well paid and often struggled to support their families.

By 1873, the family had moved to their seventh residence, this one on Sutton Street.[12] This year proved to be disastrous. In the spring, young Mary and her brother Charles contracted rheumatic fever. Although Mary recovered, with a damaged heart, Charles had a more severe case. In May 1873, he was admitted to the state almshouse in Tewksbury, suffering from St. Vitus Dance, a complication of rheumatic fever that causes rapid, jerking movements of the face, hands and feet. The almshouse entry describes his plight: "41066—McNutt Chas. H. 14 fr. Lynn. May 28, 1873. b. Lynn. always resided there. Fa. Jacob McNutt resides at 18 Central Ave. Blacksmith works for Toomey. No prop. can't tell about taxes. a native of Nova Scotia. mo. Sarah & 3 sis at home. mo. an invalid & eldest sis. has spinal disease. He has St. Vitus Dance. in bad shape."[13]

Charles died in the almshouse in June. In early August, Sarah McNutt died of kidney failure soon after the birth of her ninth child. The baby died a week later of cholera. By the end of 1873, only four of the McNutt children—Lydia, Georgianna, Ruth and Mary—were still alive.[14]

Cholera and rheumatic fever were two of many contagious diseases that swept through towns and cities in the nineteenth century. The worst outbreaks were in overcrowded areas with poor sanitation. Cholera bacteria (*Vibrio cholerae*) is transmitted by water or food that is contaminated with feces. Symptoms of the disease include severe diarrhea and dehydration, which, at that time, often led to death. Rheumatic fever, a complication of strep throat, mainly affected children. Damage to heart valves, like in Mary's case, sometimes happened after contracting the disease just once but usually occurred after repeated attacks.[15]

Nineteenth-century Lynn was crowded, with noisy markets and narrow cobbled streets traveled by horses and carts and littered with horse dung. Street-side butchers and fish vendors threw innards and meat scraps into street gutters, and residents of tenement buildings put refuse on the sides of roads. Before indoor toilets, people used shared outdoor privies and bathed infrequently. Dung heaps were commonly located close to public wells, often contaminating drinking water.

It wasn't until 1870 that sanitary conditions improved in Lynn. In that year, the Lynn Public Water Board built Breeds Pond Reservoir and began to lay pipes along city streets. By 1879, sewer lines had been laid along all but about seven miles of the major streets, but residents in houses along minor streets were still using privies with cesspools.

Jacob McNutt did not fare well after his wife died. He became a heavy drinker while continuing his pattern of frequently moving his family. The Lynn Board of Overseers of the Poor became aware that Jacob was abusing his children and, following an inspection, ordered both Mary and Ruth to be sent to the Lynn Almshouse. Jacob left nine-year-old Mary at the almshouse in September 1878 and brought her older sister Ruth the following year.[16]

When Mary and Ruth arrived at the almshouse, it consisted of two buildings—an older building with fifty poor and disabled men and women and a children's home with nine children, including Mary and Ruth. The older building had poor plumbing and rooms that were hot with little ventilation in summer. Conditions in the newer children's home were better,

Lynn Almshouse in about 1890. Mary McNutt Bailey and her father, Jacob McNutt, died here in 1888 and 1897, respectively. *Lynn Public Library.*

although money to run the facility was always short, and expenses for fuel, food and clothing were kept to a minimum.

Like other almshouses, the Lynn Almshouse had a superintendent or "keeper" and a matron, usually his unpaid wife. There was a public school next to the almshouse, which the children attended, ensuring that they received some formal education. When Ruth was fifteen, she left the almshouse and, two years later, married Henry Stiles, a stonemason. Mary left the almshouse soon after her sister and went to work as a housekeeper for a local family. Within a few months, fourteen-year-old Mary met George Bailey.[17]

After George and Mary were married, they moved with Jacob McNutt to Wiscasset, Maine, near Bailey's family in Alna. George rented a shop in the town center and set up a blacksmith shop on the ground floor with lodgings above. While Jacob worked in the shop, George found work that often took him out of town, selling goods or fixing farm equipment.

George Bailey's first child, Alice May Powers, in about 1909 with her son, Richard Edward Powers, and daughter, Ethel May Powers. *Mary Lou Bailey.*

In June 1884, George and Mary's first child, Alice May, was born, and two years later, on the same day and month, they had a second child, Una Maud. In early 1887, George returned from a trip to fix a threshing machine and found that Jacob and Mary had packed up and returned to Massachusetts, taking the children with them. According to Bailey's brother Henry, "George said that he would not go after Mary, he wasn't going to chase anybody, and he went on with his work until spring."

His brother Ben told a similar story, "George did not want to desert his business and concluded that, if his wife wanted to leave him, she could, and he did not propose to stop her."[18]

Mary had ample reason to leave Bailey. Her aunt later told the press that Mary had not gotten along with Bailey's sisters Rachel and Frances and had left Wiscasset to get away from them. But there were other reasons for Mary to leave. She was not well. Her childhood bouts with rheumatic fever had left her with a damaged heart, resulting in chronic fatigue and shortness of breath. She was struggling to care for her two children with little help from Bailey, who was often away from home, and she hoped that her family in Lynn would help her.

However, when Mary arrived in Lynn about March 1887, she found that she could not stay with her sister Ruth and her husband, Henry Stiles, because they were mourning the loss of their infant son, and this within a year of losing another son. She also could not stay with her father because he had moved to Chelsea, a city adjacent to Boston, to work as a horseshoer and did not have enough room or money to house and support Mary and her children.[19]

Mary found a place to stay in the Wyoma area of Lynn, but her health did not improve, and she and the children soon moved to the Lynn Almshouse. In April 1888, Mary, only eighteen years old, died of valvular heart disease. She was buried at Pine Grove Cemetery in Lynn. Two-year-old Una remained at the almshouse, and four-year-old Alice was transferred to the nearby Lynn Home for Children.[20]

Abbie Hilton

After Mary left, Bailey continued to work in the blacksmith shop in Wiscasset. In October 1887, twenty-three-year-old Abbie Hilton began living with him, ostensibly as his housekeeper, in his rooms above the shop. Abbie was the third of five children born to Sarah and Thomas Hilton, a day laborer. Her father died when she was five, and her mother remarried a carriage maker, Leroy Young. The Youngs moved into a house about a mile south of Wiscasset in an area called Birch Point and, in 1877, had a child, Susanna May, whom they called Susie.

By February 1888, four months after Abbie moved in with Bailey, she was pregnant. This was not good news for either of them, as Bailey was still married to Mary. However, this finally spurred Bailey to travel to Lynn to find out the fate of Mary and the two children. In late May, he traveled by steamship and rail to Lynn, but Mary had died a month earlier. He told the Lynn Board of Overseers of the Poor that he regretted that Mary had been obliged to go to the almshouse and got permission to take custody of his two daughters, Alice and Una. Bailey had his wife's body removed from Pine Grove Cemetery in Lynn and reburied in Whitefield, Maine, at a plot separate from the Bailey family plot.[21]

When George Bailey returned to Wiscasset in 1888 with Alice and Una, most townspeople assumed that he and Abbie had married, but there is no marriage record. Married or not, it was not a happy union. They quarreled frequently, and Bailey's two children by his first wife were the usual cause.[22]

In October, Abbie gave birth to Charles Thomas. By this time, Bailey was driving a mail stage the fifteen-mile distance between Wiscasset and East Boothbay. There were constant complaints about his cruelty to the horses, and within a year, he was fired.

This pattern of cruelty to animals was to continue for years. A farmhand, Denis Griffin, who met Bailey ten years later, described Bailey as "a stingy fellow of a most savage disposition, and one of the most brutal men toward horses and catle [sic] that I have ever seen. I have seen him belabor his horse most cruelly with the handle of a pitchfork. I have seen him prod cattle in the pastures with the tines of the pitchfork. Not an animal on his farm but feared him."[23] Beyond his ill treatment of animals, Bailey was generally known in Wiscasset as a brutal and violent man. The *Boston Globe* reported:

> *Bailey's life here* [in Wiscasset] *was a constant turmoil of excitement and furnished a fruitful source of gossip for the townspeople. He had a reputation while here of being a brutal, revengeful man of fierce and ungovernable temper, exceedingly quarrelsome and looked upon as a notorious thief. Anything missing about the town was sure to be charged to George E. Bailey and, as all of the natives expressed it, he would steal anything from firewood up. On account of Bailey's size and strength, there*

were very few who dared to pick a quarrel with him and, as a result, he did about as he pleased in town.[24]

After being let go as a mail-stage driver, Bailey went back to work in the blacksmith shop. In October 1890, Abbie gave birth to another son, George Edward Jr., but their lives remained in turmoil. The town was buzzing with rumors that the two little girls from Bailey's first marriage were being mistreated. People had heard that Abbie "used to beat the children and once had burned them."[25]

At this point, the town stepped in and forced the couple to give up the two children. Five-year-old Una was adopted by Edwin Seekins, a local clothing store worker, and his wife, Annie. Seven-year-old Alice was sent to the Maine Industrial School for Girls in Hallowell, which described itself as "a home for the friendless, neglected and vagrant children of the State, where, under the genial influence of kind treatment, and physical and moral training, they may be won back to ways of virtue and respectability, and fitted for positions of honorable self-support, and lives of usefulness."[26]

In April 1891, Bailey was arrested for "enticing a married woman from her home" and spent a night in the Wiscasset jail. Known as the "1812 Jail," this was the first jail built in Maine with individual cells. There were twelve granite-slab cells, six on the first floor and six on the second. The cell walls were over forty inches thick, and the only source of light was through one or two heavily barred window slits. Potbellied stoves at the end of each floor provided heat. The third story held debtors, women prisoners and those considered to be insane.[27]

A few months later, Bailey was back in jail, this time with Abbie. In November 1891, he was arrested for "affray and adultery," and two days later, Abbie was arrested for threatening to kill Bailey. According to the *Boston Globe*, "Abbie armed herself with a huge carving knife, and lay in wait for him at the gate of the house. The village doctor passing by discovered her there and persuaded her to give up the weapon."[28] For the offense of adultery, Bailey spent six months, until May 1892, in the Wiscasset jail. Over the same time, Abbie served seven months on the jail's third floor. In June 1892, she was released by "taking poor convicts oath and giving note to coal," which meant that she made a declaration of poverty and a promise to pay an overdue bill for coal.[29]

Almost as soon as Abbie was released, she found out that she was pregnant, and in January 1893, she gave birth to a son who died within a few days. She was arrested again on August 3, 1893, for "assault with intent to kill" Bailey

NAMES.	PLACE OF ABODE.	TIME OF COMMITMENT.	FOR WHAT CAUSE.
George E. Bailey	Wiscasset	9th April 1891	Enticing a married woman from her home
Abby E. Bailey	Wiscasset	19th November 1891	Threatening to kill
Abby E. Bailey	Wiscasset	31st August 1893	Assault with intent to kill

George Bailey and his wife, Abbie Hilton Bailey, both served time on multiple occasions at Wiscasset's 1812 Jail. *Photograph: authors' collection; Jail records: Lincoln County Historical Association.*

and was released on bail after serving eleven days in the Wiscasset jail. Just three months later, she was rearrested and charged with assault and battery. Though she was pregnant again, Abbie was imprisoned for eight months.[30] In January 1894, she gave birth to Sarah Emma "Sadie" in jail and was released in July. Amazingly, Bailey and Abbie continued to have children. Ethel Cynthia was born in March 1895, followed by Reta Jane in June 1897.[31]

One of their worst arguments occurred within a few hours of Abbie giving birth to Reta Jane. According to the *Boston Globe*, "They had a violent quarrel, culminating in Bailey seizing his wife on the bed where she lay and throwing her out of the window to the sidewalk beneath. The neighbors were obliged to come to her aid and carry her indoors."[32]

Susie Young

It was no secret in Wiscasset that Bailey was chasing other women, but there was one woman on whom he had set his sights: Abbie's half-sister Susie Young, who was twelve years Abbie's junior. Bailey had seen Susie over the years on trips to see Abbie's mother, Sarah, and stepfather, LeRoy Young. Bailey became friendly with LeRoy, and the two would sit together and chat over drinks. When Bailey first met Susie, she was only eleven years old. As time went by and his relationship with Abbie soured, his visits to the Youngs' house were more to see Susie than Leroy, a fact that he was careful to hide from Susie's father.[33]

By 1896, Susie was nineteen years old and returning Bailey's affection. She was a small woman with a chubby face and dark brown wavy hair, which she gathered into a bun with hairpins. Her habit of looking directly at people with her large blue eyes gave her an air of sincerity and honesty. That year, Susie began to spend nights at the blacksmith shop. While Abbie and the children occupied rooms upstairs, Susie and Bailey shared a side room on the ground floor. However, Abbie did not quietly allow her husband to carry on with her halfsister. She was a jealous woman with a temper matching that of her husband, and rather than accommodation, revenge was on her mind. As later reported in the *Boston Globe*:

> *While Bailey ran the blacksmith's shop his wife one night discovered him in the shop with one of the young women of the town. She notified some of the men of the town, and it was determined to teach Bailey a lesson. A crowd of 20 men collected, and going to the door of the shop, demanded admittance. The door of the shop was locked, and one of the mob was sent to procure an ax. Meanwhile, Bailey had harnessed his horse to his sleigh, which stood on the floor of the shop, and bundled the woman into the sleigh, covering her with robes. The moment the door was broken down Bailey sprang into the sleigh, and, lashing the horse through the crowd, disappeared up the road leading from the town before the onlookers had recovered from their surprise.*[34]

Abbie had intended to publicly humiliate both Bailey and Susie. However, the incident did not shake Susie's devotion to Bailey, and they began to talk about running off together. One night, Bailey took his wagon and drove with Susie to his brother's house in Alna. When Ben answered the door, Bailey said, "Ben, I'm going to get out of here. I cannot live with Abbie any longer."

Ben replied, "I don't know as I blame you, but I would advise you not to take Susie along with you." Ben later reported that Susie had begged him to let her go with Bailey because she loved him.[35]

Things came to a head in June 1897, when Susie had a quarrel with her mother. According to the *Boston Globe*, "Susie came to George's house and George arranged to run away with her, as Susie said she was going to be arrested in the morning for assaulting her mother. Before leaving Wiscasset, George asked his brother Henry to give Abbie some money, about eighteen or twenty dollars. Then he and Susie took the next train to

Sketch of Susie Young from the *Boston Post*, October 19, 1900. *Boston Public Library.*

Boston. When Henry went to see Abbie, she said, "If I get my eyes on that ——, I'll fix her," meaning Susie.[36]

About a week later, Henry Bailey received a letter from Boston, asking him to send some of Susie's clothes. Several years later, he told a *Boston Globe* reporter, "I never answered the letter as I did not intend to mix in the affair. I have not received a letter from him since." When asked if there was an arrest warrant out for George, Henry told the reporter, "There was no attempt to have either of them arrested. Susie's father and mother came to my house afterwards and said I must know where they were. I told them I did not, and Mr. Young said to me that he would give anything he could to get his daughter back again. She was his only child, and he was very fond of her. I could not tell him where his daughter was, for I did not know."[37]

THE ACCUSED

John Best

Early Life

John Courtney Best was born on April 8, 1865, in Sackville, New Brunswick, which was known for its shoe, tanning and shipbuilding industries. He was the second of eight children of Zilpha and Thomas Best, a shoemaker. John attended a one-room school until age twelve and worked on his uncle's farm during the summer months. By age seventeen, he was a shoemaker, as was his nineteen-year-old brother, Richard. They still lived at home with their younger siblings, Nettie, Christopher, William, Mabel, Charley and Minnie Maud.[38]

John was close to Nettie growing up, and they were often seen together. Later, when asked by a *Boston Post* reporter what he was like as a boy, she said:

> *He was cheery and laughing down there in his New Brunswick home and almost always good natured. He didn't have much of a temper, but he didn't like it when his things were disturbed. He would not fly up, but would think it over, and then tell the one who did it that he did not like it. He never looked to get even, however. He used to like to be outdoors. He liked the fields and the birds and the animals, and to go hunting and trapping. He used to catch muskrats and sell their pelts, and to hunt other animals. He went to school when he was about 14 or 15, and then he became the doctor's boy and went [a]round with him.*

Right: October 1900 police mugshot of John Best by Carleton Shorey. The *Boston Globe* noted the "stoical indifference" with which the suspected murderer faced the camera. *Boston Public Library*.

Below: Best's sister Nettie and her husband, William Stiles, posed for their portrait at the Ward Photography Studio, Lynn. From the *Boston Post*, March 24, 1901. *Boston Public Library*.

However, when the reporter asked if Best took any interest in the doctor's operations, she said, "No, he just didn't like that. He couldn't stand it. Why, when I was sick a little while ago, he came over to the house, and they were preparing me for an operation. He came into the room and saw them giving me ether, and bolted right out, and way out to the street, and didn't come back."[39]

About 1885, nineteen-year-old Nettie met William Stiles, who lived in Amherst, Nova Scotia, five miles from Sackville. The following year, they moved to Lynn, Massachusetts. In Lynn, Stiles found a job as a shoe laster, fastening the upper part of shoes to the inner soles. By this time, much of shoe manufacturing was performed by machine, but lasting remained difficult to do by machine. In October 1887, Nettie and William Stiles were married.[40]

Meanwhile, John Best had become a farmer, working for a neighbor. After this, he had a series of jobs. For about a year, he worked in a shoe factory and then worked about four months at a grocery store driving the butcher's wagon and selling cuts of meat from house to house. Following this, he drove a hackney coach, pulled by a team of horses, between the Brunswick House hotel and Sackville train station.[41]

In 1891, Best, now twenty-six, was working as a farmer again and still living in Sackville with his parents and siblings William, Mabel and Minnie Maud. His younger brother Charley had died before reaching the age of twelve. In April, Nettie traveled alone from Lynn to Sackville with her infant son Earle. She was happy to see that her favorite brother, John, had become a strong and handsome man. She described him as being about five feet six inches tall and 160 pounds, with "a ruddy face, medium complexion, slightly bald, and altogether a good-looking farmer."[42] Nettie told Best that businesses in Lynn were thriving, with plenty of jobs, especially for shoemakers. After a few weeks, he decided to join his sister.

Life in Lynn

In Lynn, Best moved in with Nettie and William Stiles in their rented house at 22 Burchstead Place and started a job as a heel-maker for the J.B. Renton Company on Broad Street. This company made "heels and cut top-pieces and spring lifts" and was an "extractor of grease from leather." Best was a good worker, and the foreman, William Conway, a burly Irishman from County Donegal, said that during the four years that Best worked for him, he "did not remain away over a week at a time."[43]

However, after Best had lived nearly four years with his sister's family, William Stiles was no longer willing to share his home and urged Best to move into one of the many rooming houses for factory workers in Lynn. In 1895, Best moved to a rooming house on Silsbee Street. The next year, he moved to another rooming house on Union Street and, in 1897, moved again to a rooming house on School Street owned by William Foote.

Foote had hired a young landlady to manage his building, and Best was soon seeking her attention. Best offered to be her handyman and do odd jobs. When she visited relatives in Maine, he collected the rent from each boarder and gave the money to Foote. But Best had begun to drink heavily. Although known about town as a generally quiet man with great self-control, he was a different man when he drank—vindictive and cruel.

In June 1898, during one of his drinking sprees, Best "had trouble" with a fellow boarder at Foote's rooming house, a shoemaker named Edward Coolley. One evening, Best waited until Coolley left the house and followed him to West Baltimore Street. He then knocked Coolley down and kicked him, leaving him unconscious. Best's boot struck Coolley on one ear as he lay on the ground, an assault that left Coolley partially deaf.[44]

Three months later, Best was involved in a more serious incident. One night, as he was retiring for bed, Foote heard a woman scream from a room on an upper floor. Foote quickly donned some clothes and ran up the stairs. Forcing the door open, he found Best in the act of assaulting the landlady. Foote grappled with Best and managed to hustle him downstairs and push him onto the street. Foote saw no more of him that night. The next day, he told the landlady to tell Best to move out.

Best moved out but soon came back to ask the landlady to allow him to return. He promised to stop drinking and to treat her kindly, but she refused. As Foote later recalled, Best came to the house one evening and asked to meet the woman on the piazza. She agreed, but when they met, Best threatened to shoot her with a revolver if she did not take him back to room in the house.

A few days later, Foote came home from his club at about 9:00 p.m. and, as usual, walked to the rear of the rooming house to lock the toolshed. However, this night he sensed that someone was there. Squeezing through a narrow passage between two buildings with a lantern in hand, Foote saw Best standing there wearing a white canvas coat and holding the collar high to obscure his face. Foote recognized the coat as one that he kept in his toolshed. He shouted, and Best reached forward and smashed the lantern. Best then hit Foote hard on the left shoulder. Stunned, Foote called out for help. Within minutes, several men responded and began to search for Best, who had jumped a fence and ran down Union Street.

At first, Foote thought that he had been hit by a brick, but in the morning, he found that the blow had come from a large claw hammer from his toolshed. He went to the police to report the assault and claimed that the force of the blow was so great that if the hammer had hit him on the head, he would probably be dead. On September 27, 1898, Best was arraigned in the Lynn Police Court and sentenced to four months in the Salem House of Correction, popularly known as the Salem jail.[45]

Best's version of the story was quite different. In October 1900, he told a *Boston Globe* reporter:

> *I used to board at his* [Foote's] *house and there was a girl that went around with me a good deal. One night after I had left the house, I went up to look in the kitchen window to see the girl who worked there. Foote didn't want me around the house and told the girl to keep me away. That night, someone told him I was in the yard and he came out looking for me. He had a lantern and I picked up a hammer and broke it. Then I ran away. I did not hit Foote. I was arrested afterward and sent away for four months.*[46]

After being released from jail in early 1899, Best moved back with his sister Nettie. Despite his criminal record, Best had a reputation of being a skilled shoemaker and was soon hired by shoe-heel manufacturer, J.G. Brown Company. When his former boss at the J.B. Renton Company, William Conway, heard that he had taken a job at Brown's, he sought out Best and offered him his old job.

In May 1899, Best was working for the Renton Company again.[47] From the day he began, he heard grumblings from other workers that their pay, which at eight dollars a week was the same as Best's, was not enough to put food on the table or allow a fellow to have a drink at a bar. In June, three company workers went on strike, demanding that their pay be raised to nine dollars a week.

Lynn had seen waves of strikes since 1860, when the city's shoe workers, demanding higher wages, had staged the largest strike the country had ever experienced. However, by 1899, the life of a factory worker had not greatly improved. The workday of both male and female workers was still longer than eight hours, often exceeding sixty hours a week. Working conditions were dangerous, social divides between laborers and management were deep and workers faced a legal system that gave them no rights but the ability to quit their jobs. Judges generally took the side of employers, and the police did not hesitate to use violence to suppress dissent.

Not much had improved in employer-worker relations by 1899. Predictably, the Renton company saw no reason to cave to worker demands and simply hired new men to replace the three striking workers. In response, fifty more men, including Best, joined the strike. However, instead of putting pressure on management, all were fired.[48]

During his trial for murder a few years later, Best was asked what he did after being let go. He replied, "Well, I loafed, I believe, a number of weeks, was stopping with my sister at the time; and she was taking vegetables—got her vegetables from a young man in East Saugus by the name of Nourse, George Nourse, and he came up to the house one day, and I told him that I was loafing—And I asked him if he knew any farmers around that—Well, he told me about—I went out to see George E. Bailey at North Saugus." When asked the date of that visit, he said, "I can't just remember, I think, though, it was about the twentieth day of July, in '99." As it would turn out, this meeting between two men, John Best and George Bailey, with clashing characters and violent tempers, ultimately sealed the fates of both.[49]

3
THE SETTING

I n June 1897, George Bailey and Susie Young arrived in Boston from Wiscasset, Maine, and took the next train to Lynn. Bailey immediately sent a letter to his friend in nearby Saugus, Henry Mitchell, to ask if he could work on his pig farm, where he had worked fifteen years earlier. Mitchell agreed to hire Bailey and invited him and Susie, who Bailey falsely claimed to be his wife, to stay at his farm. Mitchell's son Johnnie, who worked as a butcher in Saugus, and his housekeeper, Annie Dyer, also lived at the farm.[50] George and Susie stayed with Mitchell until October, when Mitchell heard that three Lynn businessmen were looking for someone to manage their farm just a mile down the road. It sounded like the perfect job for George Bailey.

Three Businessmen from Lynn

Attorney Benjamin Johnson, banker Micajah Clough and shoe manufacturer John Bartlett were prominent businessmen in Lynn who became friends in the 1880s. By that time, Lynn, like other cities, had become crowded and polluted. To escape the foul conditions, many wealthy men built rustic retreats along lakes and rivers in wilderness areas, many in New Hampshire and Maine. But Johnson had a different plan. He had grown up in Saugus and knew of a hilly, forested area known as the Six Hundred Acres. The land was mostly used for wood supplies and animal enclosures but also included an eighteen-acre farm near the southeast border owned by Edward Edmands.

Johnson thought the Six Hundred Acres would be a perfect location for a hunting and fishing retreat. In 1891, he convinced his friends Clough and Bartlett to join him in forming the Breakheart Hill Forestry Company, which would serve as a vehicle for purchasing the land. They would call their property Breakheart Hill forest, using the name of a hill in the Six Hundred Acres that colonial settlers had named after a hill in Gloucestershire, England.[51]

Johnson, Clough and Bartlett set about buying as many of the six hundred acres as possible from local owners, who were mostly yeoman farmers and shoemakers.[52] They also bought Edmands's farm by paying him $1 and assuming the remaining $1,600 on his mortgage, and they renamed the farm Breakheart Hill farm.[53] They cleared trees and brush in the forest for bridle paths to ride their beloved horses and built earthen dams across the marshes in the center of the property to create two lakes. They commissioned a nearby fish hatchery to stock the lakes with small-mouthed bass and pickerel. For gatherings of their friends, they built a log cabin–style hunting lodge, which they called Breakheart Hill camp, just north of the farm near the eighteenth-century Old Highway that ran along

The gate and warning sign at the entrance to Breakheart Hill forest in 1915. *Judith Loubris McCarthy*.

the eastern boundary of their property. In early 1896, they installed a gate at the border between the farm and the forest and mounted a warning sign on the gate that read: "This Passageway is Private Property—No Passing Through."[54] Finally, they hired a local farmer, George Parrot, to be a caretaker of the property, with an agreement that he would live at Breakheart Hill farm, keep trespassers out of the forest, harvest crops and maintain a small dairy.

Breakheart Hill Farm

The eighteen-acre Breakheart Hill farm included a red saltbox-style farmhouse, a large shingle-sided barn, an apple orchard and several acres of crops and hayfields. The farmhouse and barn, located at the top of Forest Street in Saugus, were built about 1771 by Nathan Hitchings on land that he had inherited from his father, Daniel. The elder Hitchings had owned an adjoining farm a short distance down Forest Street, which was built in the late 1600s by his grandfather, also named Daniel Hitchings, one of the area's original settlers from England.[55]

Breakheart Hill farmhouse. George Bailey converted the shed at right to a blacksmith shop. This is a 1935 photograph by the Metropolitan District Commission (MDC). *Massachusetts Department of Conservation and Recreation.*

Breakheart Hill barn, built in 1771 and razed in February 1973. This is a 1942 photograph by the MDC. *Massachusetts Department of Conservation and Recreation.*

Rear of the Breakheart Hill farmhouse, as viewed from the barn. From the *Boston Post*, October 25, 1900. *Boston Public Library.*

Nathan and his wife, Abigail, raised several children on Breakheart Hill farm and lived there for almost sixty years. In 1834, Artemas Edmands bought the farm for $400. He and his wife, Margaret, lived there for over forty years, raising three sons and an adopted daughter. Their grandson, Edward, inherited the farm, but had little interest in being a farmer. And so, when the three Lynn businessmen approached Edward to buy the property, he was happy to hand them the remaining $1,600 mortgage.

The farmhouse had two floors. The ground level had a kitchen with a dining area, sitting room, bedroom and storeroom. The second story had two small bedrooms under a gabled roof. The large, two-story barn sat just west of the farmhouse. The upper level had a large entrance with double doors that opened onto Forest Street. This level contained stalls for four horses and seven cows and a room for storing grain. Above this was a hayloft under a pitched roof, topped with a copper weathervane in the shape of a cow. The lower level, or cellar, contained a pigpen, barrels of grain, a wooden plow with a steel blade, a two-wheeled cart and a farm wagon. A side door opened from the cellar onto a wooden walkway leading to the back of the farmhouse.

George Bailey Moves to the Farm

In 1897, George Parrot left Breakheart Hill farm, and the Lynn businessmen began looking for another caretaker. Micajah Clough asked Henry Mitchell, owner of the nearby pig farm, if he knew any farmhands who might be interested in running the farm. Mitchell told him that Bailey could do the job. At that time, the word of a reputable person was enough to land a position. Few employers checked the backgrounds of job seekers. Like Mitchell, Clough assumed that Susie was Bailey's wife and offered to hire Bailey for a three-year period with the possibility of an extension.[56]

Bailey and Susie were to live in the farmhouse for an annual rent of forty dollars. In exchange, Bailey would guard the forest entrance against intruders who might hunt animals, fish in the lakes or cut trees for firewood. To help with his job, Clough gave Bailey a .38-caliber Winchester rifle. Bailey was also charged with ensuring that no one enter Breakheart Hill camp. Whenever he checked on the camp or did any maintenance there, Bailey could charge the Lynn owners twenty cents an hour. They wanted it to remain a working farm, so they bought a horse, five cows and thirty chickens from Mitchell. They told Bailey that he could keep the profits from any crops, milk and eggs that he sold.

In October 1897, Bailey loaded his wagon with his and Susie's possessions and harnessed two horses to the front. He had bought one of the horses, a dark brown mare named Kit, when he first arrived at Mitchell's farm, and Mitchell had given him the second horse in lieu of his last wages.

Bailey was thirty-eight. Susie Young was only twenty and five months pregnant. She climbed into the front seat of the wagon, and Bailey climbed into the seat next to her. At a height of six feet and a weight of two hundred pounds, he was physically large in comparison to Susie.[57] He was a handsome man with cold blue eyes, a mustache and sandy hair, which he smoothed down with a lard-based pomade, giving it a shiny and slick appearance. Bailey tightened his grip on the reins, tapped his whip on the rear of one horse and set off for nearby Breakheart Hill farm.

Micajah Clough was at the farmhouse to greet them. At Clough's direction, Bailey drove his wagon into the upper level of the barn, unhitched the horses and led them into stalls. Meanwhile, Susie went into the farmhouse through the side door. Clough told Bailey that the cows and chickens would arrive the next day. They stood together looking down the hill at the apple orchard and overgrown cropland stretching to the Newburyport Turnpike, a dirt road built in 1806 to connect markets in Boston to Newburyport. After a short discussion, Clough headed back to Lynn, satisfied that his farm was in good hands.

George and Susie took the bedroom on the first floor and quickly got into routines at the farm. Each morning, Bailey got up early and fed the horses, milked the cows and collected eggs. At midmorning, he harnessed his horse, which he called "his team," to his wagon, loaded the back with several cans of milk and a large basket of eggs and headed down Forest Street.

A quarter mile down the road on the right-hand side was an old house built by Daniel Hitchens. Hannah Hawkes had resided there for sixty years and now shared it with her grandniece, Henrietta.[58] As Bailey's wagon rattled past, Hannah would appear at the side of the road, a signal for Bailey to stop and sell her some milk. He would then continue a few miles to Charles Deary's farm in the Pleasant Hills section of Saugus, where he would sell Deary the rest of his milk and eggs. Bailey's next stop was usually to a farm owned by Simon McKenna, where he would buy a side of pork, followed by a stop at a local tavern for a cherry rum.

Some days Bailey stayed in town until late afternoon. Other days he returned to the farm and rode his horse in Breakheart Hill forest, Winchester rifle in hand. Whenever he met a trespasser, he raised the rifle and threatened to shoot. One of Bailey's farmhands later claimed that he shot some of the hunters' dogs.

Susie spent much of her time in the farmhouse kitchen. Each morning, she heated a pot of water on the wood-fired stove and added potatoes and cabbage from the root cellar and the pork that Bailey bought in town. Sometimes, instead of pork, she killed a chicken. While the stew cooked, she made cornbread using cornmeal stored in the barn.

On sunny days, she walked to the orchard with a wheelbarrow to collect apples that had fallen on the ground to make cider, which she and Bailey, like other farmers, drank with most meals. In the kitchen, she fed the apples into a cider press and turned a cast-iron wheel to chop and grind them. She turned a second wheel to lower the pressing plate and squeeze out the juice, which flowed into a wooden tub beneath the press. Next, she covered the tub with a wooden lid and set it near the stove to ferment.

Kitchen in the Breakheart Hill farmhouse. From the *Boston Post*, October 26, 1900. *Boston Public Library.*

Bailey returned to the farmhouse in the evenings. He rode his horse into the barn, put the horse in a stall and locked the front door of the barn from the inside. He descended the stairs at the rear of the barn and came out through the cellar, making a clomping sound as he walked along the boardwalk to the back of the farmhouse. Entering the house through the kitchen door, he hung his lantern on a hook to the left of the door and went into the sitting room. There, he flopped down in his favorite chair, a wooden rocking chair, and leaned forward with his hands on his knees and waited for Susie to call him for supper.[59] Susie usually sat with Bailey in the dining area off the kitchen while Bailey noisily ate his stew, dipping the cornbread into the broth.

To the townspeople, George and Susie seemed like an ordinary farm couple. However, they didn't escape the notice of one man. Everett Gould had gone to school with Susie in Wiscasset. He had heard that Susie had gone off with George Bailey, a man whom he recalled "was as good a blacksmith as could be found anywhere." Gould had left Wiscasset to take a job on the Lynn and Boston Railroad.

One day while walking along Market Street in Lynn, he was surprised to see Susie coming out of a dry goods store. Just outside the store, she joined a man who he recognized as George Bailey. Walking over to the pair, Gould smiled and said, "Hello George. Hello Susie." But George and Susie pretended not to hear and quickly walked away. Gould wrote home and informed his friends that George Bailey and Susie Young were in Lynn.[60]

Within a month of moving to the farm, Bailey realized that if he was to earn money harvesting crops, he would need a farmhand to help him. It was still autumn, but the fields needed to be plowed to prepare for planting hay, corn, cabbages, potatoes and tomatoes in the spring.

After making some inquiries in Saugus, George hired William Whitely, a farmhand. Whitely moved into the farmhouse with George and Susie, taking a bedroom on the second floor facing the road. It was a small, cramped room under the gabled roof. Whitely plowed the fields and stayed on through the winter, helping Bailey chop wood for the stove and do repairs on the 130-year-old farmhouse and barn. But by early March 1898, he was no longer willing to wait to be paid and could no longer endure living on the farm.

By this time, the household included baby Franklin, born in the farmhouse on Valentine's Day. When Whitely left, he claimed that Bailey owed him forty dollars for five months of work and that Bailey had given him only a single suit of clothes and a few more things worth no more than eighteen dollars.

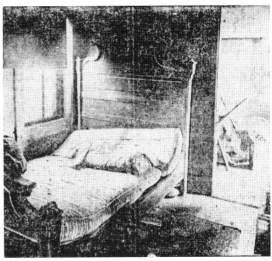

Top: Sitting room in the Breakheart Hill farmhouse, with Bailey's armchair at right. From the *Boston Post*, October 25, 1900. *Boston Public Library.*

Bottom: Bedroom used by George Bailey and Susie Young. Their child, Franklin, was born in this room in February 1898. From the *Boston Post*, October 26, 1900. *Boston Public Library.*

Two years later, Whitely described himself to a *Boston Herald* reporter as "a hard-working man, averse to conversing with reporters" and a man who enjoyed "the reputation of being truthful." When asked whether Bailey and Susie got along, he replied, "Not very well." He went on to say that Bailey was a hard man to get along with and that while he seemed a nice man on the street and away from the farm, he was a "terror" at home.

Whitely recounted an evening when Bailey came home and the three of them ate dinner together. "Bailey did not like something that was said or done, and the woman contradicted him. She got mad, jumped up from the table, and, telling Bailey she would shoot him, tried to get the rifle, which was in an adjoining room. Bailey got hold of her before she could get the rifle, and that ended it. He then bumped her head against the door."

The reporter asked if Susie knew how to handle a rifle. "You bet she did," replied Whitely, "and she was a good shot, too. Bailey taught her how to handle the gun, because he wanted her to be able to protect herself when she was left alone on the farm. I have seen her shoot at a cat at a distance of 50 feet or more while it was crawling along the top of a wall, and she picked it off, too. Another time I saw her shoot a bulldog in the field. It took her three shots to do it, but she did it just the same."

When asked if Susie had ever expressed a desire to go back to Maine, Whitely replied, "She often told me that she would like to see her folks, but Bailey told her to put it off. He would not let her go, and, when she asked him for money to pay her fare, he always refused. He did not want her to leave the premises even for a day."

However, Susie told quite a different story about her home life with Bailey. She said, "He never spoke a cross word to me in his life, and we never had a quarrel. George Bailey was one of the best friends I ever had."[61]

In the summer of 1898, Bailey hired another man known only as "the Swede." Just over two years later, after Bailey was murdered, state officers questioned the Swede because of an incident he reported to Breakheart owner Benjamin Johnson and repeated to a *Boston Globe* reporter. As reported in the *Globe*, "Bailey assaulted him [the Swede] several times on account of his way of doing the work on the place. During one violent outburst of anger, Bailey seized a horsewhip and gave the Swede a thrashing. He then threw his clothes at him and ordered him out of the place.…The Swede left threatening vengeance on his employer."[62] However, one of the officers, George Neal, did not believe that the Swede would postpone taking revenge for over two years. Neal thought it more likely that he would have retaliated by killing Bailey on a lonely road on his milk-delivery route, burning the farm buildings, poisoning the cows or destroying crops.

Sketch of Joseph Craig, "the Spaniard." From the *Boston Post*, October 21, 1900. *Boston Public Library.*

Following the Swede's brief stay at the farm, Bailey hired more farmhands. Like the previous farmhands, these men left soon after being hired. In May 1899, Bailey hired a man from Boston, Joseph Craig, and agreed to pay him fifteen dollars a month.[63]

Craig found the experience of living and working with Bailey so disturbing that he left after only ten days. In an October 1900 interview with a *Boston Post* reporter, Craig said:

> *Bailey spent scarcely an hour upon the farm. He was usually away until about 11:30 at night, going away in a buggy to Salem or Lynn. He used to come home drunk, for I would hear the racket he made. Susie Young was living with him, and at that time I thought she was his wife. The place was too lonesome for me....I stayed on the farm for ten days, and then notified Bailey and told him not to get a man from Boston to take my place as the farm was too lonesome for a city man. Bailey jumped to his feet, very red in the face, and said: "Why I could get a man from Boston in a moment." On the next morning, Bailey took the milk to town. When he got back, I was dressed, ready to leave, and was waiting for him to pay me the $5.75 he owed me for ten days' work. He came rushing up to me with clenched fists. "You take the road," he cried, "there it is." I told him I would not go until he paid me. He refused to pay me and threatened to have me arrested. I told him to send for the officer, that I wanted to see what I would be arrested for. He up and threw open his coat, bawling out: "I am an officer. I can arrest you! Then he grabbed me by my coat, threw me on my back to the ground, put his knees to my stomach and grasped my throat with his left hand, and with his right hand marked me all up in the face, crying out with curses: "You Spaniard! Will you go now?" I replied, "No." He offered me $2 if I would go. Again, I refused; I wanted all that was owed me. Then he took me by the leg and dragged me over thirty feet down the road. Susie Young dragged my trunk out of the house and threw it on the ground and then kicked me. Then Bailey offered me $3 to quit and go, and this, too, I refused. He cried out that he would get his revolver and shoot me and ran into the house. I saw that he meant what he said, so I left the farm.*[64]

According to Craig, Bailey was "a hard drinker, a man of savage and quarrelsome disposition, and extremely niggardly in money matters." Craig also claimed that Bailey quarreled continually with Susie and kept a loaded gun in the house, which he used to threaten trespassers in Breakheart Hill forest. Craig recounted one occasion when Bailey would have killed a horse with an axe had he not stopped him.[65]

John Best Arrives at Breakheart Hill Farm

In June 1899, a month after Joseph Craig left the Breakheart property, John Best was "loafing" after being fired from the J.B. Renton Company when he heard about a job opening at Breakheart farm from a vegetable salesman. He knew nothing about the experiences of Bailey's previous farmhands when, on July 20, 1899, he rode his "wheel," which he later admitted he had stolen, to the Saugus farm to meet Bailey. Bailey liked Best right away and hired him for a month, promising to pay him fifteen dollars a week with free room and board.[66]

Best moved into the farmhouse, taking the same second-floor bedroom as the previous farmhands, and worked for a month. Near the end of that time, Bailey tried to get Best to stay longer and offered to go into partnership with him raising hens. Best told him, "I would like to first rate if I thought we could make it successful," but added that he had had enough of farming for a while. Bailey paid Best for his month's work but was still reluctant to let him go. He asked Best if, after a two- or three-day visit to Lynn, he would come back for a week or so to help bring in the marsh hay. Best responded that he could not promise, but he would if he could.

In Lynn, Best moved back in with his sister Nettie. He arrived just as they were moving from Lynn to East Saugus, where her husband, William Stiles, planned to raise hens. So, instead of returning to Bailey's farm, Best moved with his sister's family to Saugus and took a job helping a nearby farmer.[67]

In September 1899, the foreman from J.G. Brown, the shoe-heel company where Best had previously worked, stopped by the Stiles house to offer him his old job, which Best accepted. By this time, William Stiles had decided to give up raising hens and had rented a small house on Marianna Street back in Lynn. Best continued living with them and worked for J.G. Brown for a few months, and then, despite his previous involvement with strikers, was hired to work for the J.B. Renton Company again. But by March 1900, Best was out of work.

With an uncanny sense of timing, George Bailey chose the month of March to ride to Lynn to ask Best to return to Breakheart Hill farm. Surprised that Bailey would travel to Lynn on his account, Best still refused and said that, although he wasn't doing anything at present, he didn't want to go back to the Saugus farm.[68]

In April, Bailey hired Fred Burnell, a French-born farmhand from the neighboring town of Melrose. Burnell and his wife, Jeannette, who was eight

Above: Best's bedroom soon after he was arrested. This room was used by farmhands Joseph Craig and Fred Burnell before Best arrived in May 1900. From the *Boston Post*, October 25, 1900. *Boston Public Library.*

Right: William and Nettie Best Stiles lived in this house at 9 Marianna Street in Lynn. *Photograph by Douglas L. Heath.*

months pregnant, moved into Breakheart Hill farm, taking the upstairs bedroom. Over the next few weeks, Burnell helped Bailey with spring planting. But the couple soon returned to Melrose. A week later, on May 19, their son was born. Tragically, he died of "debility" less than a month later. Remaining in Melrose, Burnell continued to work part-time for Bailey.[69]

In late April, shortly before Burnell left, Bailey again drove his wagon to Lynn and asked Best to return to the farm, saying that, true to his name, he had been Bailey's best worker. He asked Best to get in the wagon and go with him directly to Breakheart Hill farm. Best again declined, saying that he had an engagement, but he would come out on his bicycle the following Sunday. On May 6, as promised, Best cycled to the Saugus farm. Bailey told Best that if he would take care of the stock and do the cultivating, he would provide him with room, board and half of whatever they raised on the farm. Best finally agreed and moved back into the second-story bedroom the following week.[70]

The summer of 1900 turned out to be poor for farming. The weather was dry, and the lack of rain stunted crop growth and resulted in low yields of hay and silage needed to feed the livestock. By July, Best told Bailey that there wasn't enough work for the two of them and that there was barely enough to pay one. He wanted to sell his share to Bailey and leave the farm. Bailey insisted that they could still get something, at least a crop of cabbage. Bailey said, "If you will stay, I will give you half of the apples—half of the crop of apples." Again, Best agreed to stay.[71]

The following March, Best testified in court that, except for one occasion, he had always had a friendly relationship with Bailey. The one occasion, he recalled, had been in July just before the peas were ripe and ready to pick.

> *I hadn't disturbed them very much and hadn't kept the weeds pulled out as much as I could; it was so dry that I hadn't disturbed the weeds, but let them grow, and there were some tall weeds that grew into the peas, and the peas clung to the weeds. He [Bailey] proposed one day after a shower to go down and pull the weeds up. I told him that if he did that he might as well pull the peas too. He got very vexed; I was milking the cows at the time, and he talked and he swung around there. It was the first time that he ever got vexed with me.*[72]

Soon after moving to the farm, Best realized that, despite Susie Young's efforts to put a good face on the situation, she was lonely and unhappy. Having few others to talk to, she began to confide in Best and revealed her secret that she and George Bailey were not married, and that Bailey had a wife and children in Maine.

Best also heard from Winfield "Winnie" Rowe, a seventeen-year-old farmhand, that the Maine police were after Bailey for abandoning his family. Rowe lived two miles away on his parents' farm and had met Bailey at Mitchell's pig farm three years previously. He often walked to Breakheart Hill farm to help Bailey with his livestock and would stay to keep Best company while Best drank whiskey and complained that Bailey owed him money.

Best and Rowe would also discuss Bailey's unusual relationship with Susie, and during one of these conversations, Rowe said that a man who he couldn't name had told him that there was a $500 reward for turning Bailey in to the Maine police. Normally, Best would have jumped at the chance to make $500, but he was afraid that if he went to the police, they would charge him with stealing the bicycle he had taken in Lynn to ride to Breakheart Hill farm and never returned, as well as the coat he had stolen from a store in Lynn and pawned.[73]

In August 1900, two Lynn police officers came to the farm looking for George Bailey to serve him notice to appear in court on a charge of selling sour milk at the corner of Breed and Lewis Streets in Lynn. When they arrived, Bailey was in the kitchen with Susie and John Best. At first sight of the officers, Best thought they were after him for his thefts. Susie later said that "Best ran upstairs, and I supposed stayed there, but when I looked for him, he was not up there. I found him near the barn, and when he came over where Bailey and myself were, he drew a long knife, the blade of which was eight inches long, and said 'he would kill any man who tried to take him.'"[74]

Bailey appeared in court as ordered and told Judge Berry that if his milk was sour it was because someone had tampered with it. He said he had enemies who were capable of doing such a thing, and he believed they had done it. Although Bailey's statement seemed like a weak excuse at the time, a month later, the judge viewed it as "highly significant."

In early September, Susie Young witnessed a quarrel between Bailey and Best. In an interview with a *Boston Globe* reporter in October, Susie recalled that Bailey had directed Best to do some work in the garden. When Bailey came home, he found that the work had not been done and scolded Best, who responded that he was doing the best he could and said, "I ain't getting any money out of this anyway."

Bailey replied tersely, "If you don't like it, you had better get out," and Best went off in a temper.

Susie added that it was fortunate that Best was sober because "I was always afraid of Best when he had been drinking and I never spoke to him then." When pressed by the reporter about what Best meant by "not getting any money," Susie said:

> *You know that Best was to be paid half of what Bailey received from the sale of the vegetables, but he was not to get anything until the crop was sold in the fall. Best was to leave then and Mr. Bailey meant to give him the money then. Mr. Bailey never gave Best any money during the time I was there. He was afraid to give him money, because he would spend it all on drink and he would be drunk until the money was gone. Whenever Best wanted anything Mr. Bailey would buy it for him. He used to buy what clothes Best wanted and he used to buy his tobacco. Best was able to get liquor once in a while. When he was drinking, he drank as long as he could get it. Once, when he had been without liquor for some time, he wanted some money, and Mr. Bailey would not give it to him. He pawned his overcoat in Lynn and spent what he got for it for whisky. When he got sober, he told Mr. Bailey about it, and Mr. Bailey paid what was due and got the coat back.*[75]

Another incident also happened in September that added credence to Susie's claim that Best was unpredictable and possibly dangerous. Robert Porter, a young farmhand living at Simmons veterinary farm less than a mile from Breakheart Hill farm, testified in court in March 1901 that he would sometimes ride his bicycle with Best. On one of these rides, Best got a flat tire, and they stopped to fix it at the East Saugus Methodist Church. Porter told Best, "You want to look out, because Bailey will knock you out."

Best replied, "I don't think so. I know how to handle them kind of people."[76]

Soon after this ride, Porter went to the Breakheart farm to buy vegetables. He recalled that "Mr. Bailey came in the house and went out. Mr. Best says to me, he says, 'Bailey hates me, but he don't like to say anything because he don't like to get rid of my work, but I am just waiting for a chance to get him out of this town.'"[77]

Another farmhand, Fred Burnell, who had briefly lived at the farm and helped Bailey mow hay, testified about a conversation he had had with Best in September 1900. Burnell told Best that Bailey hadn't paid him for three weeks, and he was thinking of going somewhere else to work. Best replied that he also had not been paid, adding, "It is pretty hard for a man not to get a few dollars when he wants it, when he has worked all summer." When

Burnell noted that he could get Best a job for fifteen dollars a month, Best replied, "I ain't going to leave the farm now, when I worked all summer on it. If I leave the farm now, I might not get my money on it." According to Burnell, Best said that Bailey "had fooled a number of young fellows, but he can't fool this chicken, because if he does, I will fix him."[78]

Susie Young Returns to Maine

Since arriving at Breakheart Hill farm, Bailey and Susie had quarreled a great deal. By September 1900, their quarreling had reached a level where they were unable to be together without exchanging harsh words. Many of the arguments started with Susie asking Bailey for money and Bailey refusing, claiming that he didn't have any. However, the following month, Best testified in court that "he did have some money, as he got $30 from Charles Leutz, the foreman of the Bennett farm, about the first of the month, for work he had done."

One night during a quarrel, Susie said, "George, I'm going home to see my folks; they are sick." It was four years since she had been home to Wiscasset.

Susie put her clothes in a barrel and got ready to go, but Bailey told her that if she waited until the end of the month, he would give her some new clothes and twenty-five dollars. She agreed to stay a little longer. Later, when alone with Best, Susie told him that she would never come back. She was afraid that Bailey's wife would come to Saugus and have her arrested.[79] She asked Best if he would write to her. He said no, so she asked him if he would answer if she wrote to him. This time he said, "Sure." The conversation continued:

"Where would I direct the letter?"

"Why, direct it to Saugus."

"I would rather not send a letter to Saugus. George always gets the mail or stops to the post office, and he would be liable to get it, and he might not like it very well if he knew I was writing to you."

"Well, under the circumstances, why, address it to my sister's in Lynn."

Susie also asked Best if he "thought it was well" to take two-year-old Franklin with her.

"No, you should not take the boy. They don't know down there among your folks that you have a boy, and if you take the boy down there, that will simply disclose that fact. I should advise you to leave the boy here somewhere with a neighbor."[80]

Instead of waiting until the end of the month, Susie decided to leave on September 27. She ignored Best's advice and took Franklin with her. According to Best:

> She did not know the night before she was going the next day, but, of course, expected to go at any time. The morning came and I was up at the barn at work. She came up to see me and said, "John, I am going to Wiscasset and I will not come back. Do you want me to write to you?" It was then that I said, "Why, certainly." Bailey came up and harnessed the horse and drove her and the baby down to the station. She went on the 9:20 train. He came right back but did not say anything about her. Sometime after, he remarked that it was funny that she did not write to him. It bothered him a great deal.[81]

Best's sister Nettie Stiles met Bailey, Susie and young Franklin at the station in Lynn and watched as the 9:20 a.m. train left for Portland, Maine. When later asked by a *Boston Post* reporter why Susie had left, Nettie replied:

> I don't know. She wanted me to come down to the depot, and I went. She asked George if he was going to write to her, and he said he was not much on writing. She said that she would write if he would answer, and he said he would try to. When Susie got on the train, George Bailey followed her into the car. I watched them, and he did not speak. If he did his lips did not move. Then I saw him look at her, and both of them were as white as sheets. Something was the matter. I don't know what it was, but it was something. After she was gone, George was glum, but said nothing. He had said before that Susie was bound to go, but Susie said, when she got to the train, that she did not care whether she went or not. She never wrote to Bailey after that, but she did write to John.[82]

On October 6, a letter from Wiscasset addressed to Best arrived at Nettie's house on Marianna Street in Lynn:

> *1900. Wiscasset, Maine, Oct 4.*
> *My Dear Friend:*
> *John, I write a few lines. I got here in safe. I got a bad cold. Can just speak out loud. I found them quite well, but all was pleased to see me. I had a lots of company since I came. We are having some rain. How is it all the folks? Hope this will find you and all well. Please write me the news and tell me*

*how you are getting along. I will not write much for I am sick and don't feel
like it. Please write soon. From your loving friend,
Susie L. Young*[83]

The next day, twenty-one-year-old Johnnie Mitchell, Henry Mitchell's
son, recalled seeing Bailey about noon that day riding in a democrat wagon
on the road to Wakefield near Castle Hill, the highest point in Breakheart
Hill forest.[84] In the afternoon, Bailey stopped by Henry Mitchell's house and
spoke briefly with his housekeeper, Annie Dwyer, before going across to the
farm with Mitchell. According to Dwyer, Bailey "came on some business
with Mr. Mitchell about some grain."[85]

Saugus farmhand Winfield
Rowe. He gave the longest
testimony of any witness
during Best's trial. About
three years later, Rowe died
in a trolley explosion in
Melrose. From the *Boston
Globe*, September 23, 1904.
Boston Public Library.

Monday, October 8, started out fair but turned
to rain in the evening. It was the last day that
anyone saw George Bailey alive. That morning,
Winnie Rowe and Bailey drove their hay wagons
together to a marsh near the Franklin Park trotters
racetrack in Saugus to mow and gather hay. Rowe
noted that Bailey had a "street blanket" on his
horse. They arrived at the marsh at about 10:00
a.m., shortly after the horse races had begun.

After cutting and loading some hay, Bailey
took out his gold watch and timed several races.[86]
It was a watch that Rowe had seen Bailey use
many times before. They finished filling their
wagons at about 3:30 p.m. and set off for home.
At 5:00 p.m., they reached a schoolhouse at the
corner of Forest and Main Streets in Saugus, at
which point Rowe headed to his family's farm
on Howard Street, and Bailey continued north
along Forest Street to Breakheart Hill farm.[87]

That evening, Bailey and Best ate a dinner of
pork, corn and tomatoes, finishing with some of
Bailey's homemade cherry rum.[88] By 8:00 p.m., it
had begun to rain heavily. Bailey put on a canvas
hat, corduroy jacket and worn, double-breasted
coat, which he buttoned down in the front. He
walked along the wooden walkway to the barn,
harnessed his dark bay mare to the democrat
wagon and loaded it with five milk cans. The

The Deary family about 1890. (*Left to right*): Annie Deary holding baby Thomas, Edward Deary (four) and Charles Deary holding James (two). Charles and Annie Deary were the last people known to see Bailey alive. *Courtesy of Brian Perry.*

spokes in the wagon wheels were so loose that the wagon made a rickety noise. Taking a kerosene lamp from the back of the wagon, he lit it with a match and hooked it to the front of the wagon. Clutching the reins, he went out into the dark, wet night. At the bottom of Forest Street, he turned left onto Main Street and headed to Charles Deary's farm in the Pleasant Hills neighborhood of Saugus.[89]

Just before 9:00 p.m., Bailey drove his wagon around the right side of Deary's farmhouse to the milk house in the rear, where Deary was waiting for him. The two men carried the milk cans up the four steps into the house. Bailey unbuttoned his coat and waited for Deary to go into the farmhouse to get money for the milk. When Deary returned to say that he didn't have the right amount, Bailey said he'd collect it on his next visit. Bailey buttoned his coat, braced himself against the driving rain, and drove back into the night.[90]

4

WHERE IS BAILEY?

Tuesday, October 9

James Thomas, a carpenter, was seventy-eight years old and in failing health, but he could still walk a mile or two. On Tuesday morning, he walked from his house on Forest Street, past Hannah Hawkes's place and up to Breakheart Hill farm to visit Bailey. It had been raining all night, and he stepped carefully to avoid slipping on mud in the rutted road. He knocked on the farmhouse door. Getting no answer, he walked around to the back and saw the smoking remnants of a bonfire between the house and the barn. Thomas took a stick and poked at the embers. Among them, he noticed a fragment about two feet long and two inches wide with a reddish cast that appeared to be part of a horse blanket. Thomas pushed the fragment into a pile with the other embers so they would burn more completely. Not finding Bailey at the house or barn, he walked to the cabbage patch to see if his farmhand, Best, might be down there, but no one was in sight.[91]

As Thomas was knocking on the door to the Breakheart farmhouse, Best was in Saugus center sitting in the democrat wagon in front of Simon McKenna's farmhouse, where his friend Johnnie Mitchell lived. He got down from the wagon and knocked on the front door. When McKenna answered, Best asked if Johnnie was home.

"I think he went up to Reading after some cows."

"What time will he be back?"

"I don't know for sure, but I don't think till the afternoon."

"You may tell him to come over to Bailey's when he comes home, I want to see him. I am Mr. Bailey's man."

"Is that so?"

"Bailey skipped out last night."

"That is kind of a funny thing. Where do you suppose he has gone?"

"I think he has gone down in Maine. He heard the officers was after him and he skipped."[92]

Best next stopped at Henry Mitchell's house to see if Johnnie was there. It began to rain again as he pulled up to the front of the farmhouse. He was glad that he had put on a waterproof glazed coat. Stepping down from the wagon, he saw Annie Dwyer, Mitchell's housekeeper, at the door and called out, "Has George been here?"

"No. Why? Haven't you seen him?"

"I have not seen him since he went away last night with his milk. It is funny and strange because he did not leave grain for the cattle. Do you know where Johnnie is?"

"Johnnie might be at Win Rowe's. Haven't you had anything to eat? If you didn't have, why, I should have you have a cup of coffee."

Best thanked her but declined. He tightened his grip on the reins, flicked the horse with his driving whip and headed west to Winnie Rowe's.[93]

Just past 9:00 a.m., Rowe's mother, Sarah, heard a wagon pulling up in her backyard and went to the door. Best sat in his team and called out, "Win! Win!" Sarah appeared at the door, and Best asked, "Is Win home?"

"No, Winnie has gone to Peabody."

"Does he know where Bailey is?"

"I think not."

"Well, Bailey has skipped."

"What do you mean? Winnie and he were just on the marsh yesterday getting hay."

"Yes, I know," Best replied. "Each of them brought home a load of hay. After that, he went with his milk."

"And didn't he come back from carrying his milk?"

"Yes, he came back from carrying his milk all right because I heard him, but I wasn't talking to him. It has left me in a bad place that there ought to be some grain got. Could you tell Winnie when he comes home to come right over?"

"I don't think he will be here until 4 o'clock."

"Well, you tell him to come over; you tell him that Bailey has skipped and I want him to come over because I don't know what to do."[94]

Not finding Johnnie or Winnie and reluctant to go back to the empty farmhouse, Best headed to Lynn. He went into several saloons, downing one or two glasses of whiskey in each. He then made his way downstairs to Keliher's Saloon in the Market Square Hotel. By noon, he was so drunk that the bartender refused to sell him any more liquor and told him to leave. Best started to go out but missed the door. Finally, the bartender escorted him out.

Instead of going to his wagon, Best waited until the bartender was busy with other customers and went back into the hotel. He stood against the bar and collapsed, but others at the bar stopped him from falling to the floor. Simon O'Brien, a pattern maker who worked for the Gallagher Manufacturing Company, was standing at the end of the bar reading a newspaper when he saw Best collapse. He and others helped Best to the street, where his horse and wagon were hitched to a post. Best was too drunk to get into the wagon without help and was unable to give them his name. O'Brien asked if anyone knew who he was; one man thought he lived in Saugus.

As the man obviously could not drive his wagon, O'Brien jumped in with him and drove to Dudley Johnson's house in East Saugus, where he thought the drunk man might be employed. When he reached the Johnson farm, there were several men standing about, but no one knew the drunken man. Johnson's son, Fred, noticed "G.E. Bailey, Saugus" written on the side of the wagon and suggested that O'Brien let go of the reins and let the horse lead him to the man's house.

Dropping the reins, the horse led O'Brien to Saugus center. The rain had not let up, and both he and Best were soaking wet. Best suddenly roused from his stupor and grabbed the reins to stop the horse. He started to get out of the wagon but slipped and fell onto the roadside. O'Brien was trying to lift him when William Perkins, a local mason, stopped to help.

Perkins knew where George Bailey lived and offered to drive the wagon while O'Brien held Best. They stopped in front of the Breakheart barn, pulled Best from the wagon and placed him upright inside the barn. They threw a blanket over the horse and went out to see if anyone was in the farmhouse. Finding the side door unlocked, they went inside and shouted but got no answer.

O'Brien had assumed that Bailey would be grateful to have his team back safely and would give him a ride home. With no choice but to walk,

O'Brien and Perkins made their way through the woods in the rain to Saugus center. Once there, Perkins turned toward his house while O'Brien took a streetcar to Lynn.

That afternoon, Johnnie Mitchell stopped by his father's farm. Annie Dwyer told him that Best had been there earlier looking for him. After doing some chores, Mitchell drove his team to Breakheart Hill farm and arrived just before sunset. Dogs were barking, and the side door of the farmhouse was slightly open. Entering, he found Best asleep in a rocking chair in the kitchen. Mitchell aroused him by saying, "Hallo John."

When Best was fully awake, Mitchell asked, "Where is George?"

"He has skipped."

"Did he say anything where he was going? Did he leave any word with you?"

"No, he didn't. All I can remember is that he went down with the milk the night before that, and he came round to my window and he says, 'Johnnie, I didn't get any paper,' and that is the last I remember of it."[95]

Mitchell noticed that Best was slightly drunk and suggested that they go out to the barn. The cows were standing outside in the rain, so they brought them in, fed them some grain, and Best began milking them. Looking up, he asked Mitchell, "What should I do with the milk?"

"You are going to take it down just the same as though George had left word with you to take it down."

"I don't know where to go with it."

"When you get them milked, you can hitch up one of the teams and drive down to where I board, and I will go down with you."

"All right," replied Best.

With that, Mitchell left Best in the barn and drove back to Simon McKenna's. When he had finished milking the cows, instead of using Bailey's democrat wagon, Best hitched a brown mare to the front of an open box buggy. He put four cans of milk in the back and headed down the road to meet Mitchell. The two men drove the short distance to Deary's farm, arriving in the early evening. Best stayed in the buggy while Mitchell jumped out to put the milk in the milk house. "Where is George tonight?" Deary asked.

"He disappeared Monday night, and we haven't seen him since. He was a little sick and it looks like he has gone on a vacation," Mitchell replied.[96] When he had finished taking the milk out of the buggy, Mitchell put some clean, empty cans in the buggy and climbed into the front. Taking the reins from Best, Mitchell drove to McKenna's farm, where he got out and watched as Best turned the horses to head home.[97]

Wednesday, October 10

James Thomas walked up to Breakheart farm again on Wednesday. The morning was cool and rainy. He found Best in the barn and asked him where Bailey had been the day before. Best told him that he didn't know and that yesterday he had gone over to Johnnie Mitchell's and to Winnie Rowe's looking for him. Thomas mentioned the bonfire. "Bailey had a fire up there," replied Best. "After Susie Young went off, he gathered up a lot of stuff that had accumulated in the house and had burned it out there in that passageway."

Looking around, Thomas saw that all four horses, including Bailey's, were in the barn. When he mentioned this, Best told Thomas that he had gone to the barn that morning and found the horse in his stall and the harness hung on the proper pegs. He thought that Bailey was in the house and, after finishing his chores, had gone in to find him, but Bailey was not there. Best added that he was going to Lynn that night to see his sister Nettie to find out whether she had heard anything or knew anything about Bailey. He also wanted to get some money out of his brother-in-law to get some oats for the horses.[98]

After Thomas left, Best sat at the kitchen table and wrote a short reply to Susie's letter to let her know that he had received her letter and that Bailey had "skipped." He hitched a horse to the democrat wagon and drove to Saugus center to mail it. As Best was driving past Simon McKenna's on Main Street, McKenna waved for him to stop. "Have you seen George?" he asked.

"No, I have not," Best replied. "I wrote a note down to Susie Young to see if George was down there. I'm in a hurry to catch the mail and get back home in case some of the campers come up to camp." Best was referring to Breakheart Hill camp, where prominent men from Lynn often went to hunt or fish or simply to socialize. With Bailey and Susie gone, Best now had the job of making sure that the camp was in good order.[99]

That afternoon, Winnie Rowe walked two miles from his house to Breakheart Hill farm. Seeing the barn door open, he went inside. Best was not there, so he went into the house and found him sitting in the kitchen holding a whiskey bottle. Rowe asked where Bailey was. Best replied, "I don't know. I last saw him when he went away with the milk." After a pause, he continued, "I didn't hear him come home, but when I went out there in the morning the team was there and the horse. Let's look in his bedroom and see if he's there." Best pulled the covers off the bed, then bent down and looked under the bed. They then looked through Bailey's clothes and noted that he had left his fur coat behind.

Returning to the kitchen, Best took the .38-caliber Winchester rifle off a hook above the ice chest and removed it from its canvas case. He went into the living room and loaded four or five cartridges in it, went outside and fired at a box about thirty feet away. "I'm going to hit that knot on the side of the box," said Best and shot again, missing the knot by a half inch. As he turned back toward the house holding the rifle, Rowe quickly moved behind him. "Are you afraid I was going to shoot you?" he asked.

"No, I wasn't afraid of that," Rowe said with a nervous laugh. Best gestured toward a post on the side of a gate and said he was going to hit it about an inch down from the top. He hit it right on the mark. Satisfied, he rubbed the barrel of the rifle on the side of his foot. The gun suddenly went off, and a bullet nearly hit him in the foot. Shaken, Best went into the house and put the gun back above the ice chest.

From the farmhouse, Best and Rowe saw Robert Porter, a young farmhand, mowing hay on the neighboring farm. Looking up, Porter called for them to come down. On the way, Best told Rowe not to say anything about Bailey being gone. Best walked ahead, while Rowe lagged behind picking up apples. When Best reached the stone wall separating the farms, Porter could see that he had been drinking and said, "Drunk, eh?"

Best replied, "Yes, and got money, too." He put his hand in his pocket and pulled out some bills and waved them at Porter before stuffing them back into his pocket.[100]

At that moment, Denis Griffin, an older farmhand who had hired Porter, appeared, and Porter went back to work. Griffin climbed over the wall and joined Best and Rowe as they headed back up the hill.

As they walked, Griffin said, "I was just down at Hannah Hawkes' house and she told me that Bailey has run away."

"Yes, he has skipped," replied Best.

Reaching the farmhouse, Best took a bottle of whiskey out of the ice chest and invited Griffin in to have a drink with him, but Griffin said, "No, that's not the kind I drink. I'd better be getting home."

"Suit yourself," replied Best and took a long swig.

After Griffin left, Best and Rowe had supper, milked the cows and loaded the milk into the democrat wagon to take to Deary's farm. As they were getting into the wagon, Rowe asked, "Where are those two street blankets that used to be here?"

"I don't remember any such street blankets."

Surprised that he didn't remember, Rowe said, "We had one of them down to the marsh on Monday."

"Well, Bailey might be up in the hay with a blanket to cover him over."

As Best said this, Rowe realized that they hadn't checked the hayloft. He quickly climbed up but found only hay. When he came down, Best was holding an old stable blanket and asked Rowe if that was the blanket he was talking about. Rowe said that it appeared to be and got in the wagon, giving the matter no more thought.

They passed James Thomas as they were driving down Forest Street. He waved for them to stop and called to Best, "Do you know who drove the team home Monday night? If we only knew who brought the horse back, we should know pretty near where Bailey was." Best replied that he didn't know and that he hadn't heard the team that night. He then flicked his driving whip and urged the horse on.[101]

It was dusk and beginning to rain when they left Deary's farm, but instead of returning to Breakheart Hill farm, they went on to Lynn. First, Best stopped at Keliher's liquor store and bought a pint bottle of whiskey. Farther on, he stopped at a market and came out with a quart of peanuts, a new TD pipe and some tobacco.[102]

Reaching Lynn, Best went into Frank Dolan's Saloon on Union Street for a drink while Rowe stayed in the wagon. From there, Best went to Nettie's house. Rowe declined to go in, and Best returned almost an hour later and said that his brother-in-law, William Stiles, had agreed to buy eggs from Best the next day so that he could buy grain for the livestock.

On the way back to Breakheart Hill farm, Rowe stopped the wagon at Best's request at two more bars and again at Keliher's. Rowe waited outside while Best went into the saloon and emerged later holding two pints of whiskey. He was accompanied by another man, Arthur Jordan, who had asked Best for a lift to Raddin's Court, a road along their way. Climbing into the front of the wagon, Best opened one of the pints and began drinking from it, biting off the end of his pipe between swigs. When they reached Raddin's Court, instead of stopping, Best took the whip from Rowe and used it on the horse to speed it up. He turned to Rowe and said he was taking Jordan to Breakheart farm to stay the night. Best then, without reason, hit Rowe in the face with the whip.

As Best drove, he kept taking bites off the end of his pipe. On reaching the Saugus cemetery, when he seemed at his drunkest, he tossed the pipe onto the road. Soon after, he turned to Rowe and asked him where his TD pipe was. Rowe replied, "I don't know where it is." Best thought a moment and said, "Oh, yes; I threw it away up there by the cemetery."

Best stopped at the end of the road to Rowe's parents' farm to drop him off. He turned to Jordan and asked him to stay overnight with him at Breakheart farm because he was lonely and wanted company. But Jordan refused and gruffly told Best to take him to North Saugus so he could take a streetcar home. As the horse was worn out from the frantic ride, Best stopped first at Breakheart farm and harnessed another horse before the two men made their way through the woods along the dark road toward North Saugus.

Along the way, they rattled noisily past Albert Day's farm. Later, during Best's arraignment for murder, Albert Day and his wife told the police that on that night they were awakened by a dog barking. They heard the noise of wagon wheels rumbling over the stones on the road. Mrs. Day looked out of window but could see nothing through the mist, although they both heard a wagon being driven rapidly over the nearby bridge.[103]

Thursday, October 11

The next morning, Johnnie Mitchell decided to drive to Breakheart Hill farm to check on Best. He knocked on the kitchen door several times before trying to open it. It was locked, but the storeroom door was open. Finding no one on the ground floor, he went upstairs and found Best in bed, awake and fully dressed. Mitchell smiled and said, "Good morning, it's time to get up and do your chores." Best grunted in response. Mitchell turned and went back downstairs and out to the barn. A few minutes later, Best joined him.

"Have you heard or seen anything of Bailey," Mitchell asked.

"No, and there isn't any grain or anything for the cattle and stock."

"Why don't you go and get some?"

"I don't have any money."

"Well, it would be a good idea for me to go and get some and I guess the camp owners Johnson or Clough will pay me."

Instead of replying, Best started to milk one of the cows. Mitchell murmured, "Well then, goodbye," jumped in his wagon and drove to his father's house to tell him that he was concerned about "the condition of things over there."[104] Henry Mitchell agreed that things were bad and encouraged his son to talk with Breakheart owner Micajah Clough.

Taking his father's advice, Johnnie set out for Lynn and went directly to Clough's elegant house on Ocean Avenue, where he found his wife, Harriet, at home. Harriet listened intently as Mitchell told her that Bailey had apparently left for Maine, leaving only his farmhand, who was not able to manage on his own. Harriet asked about Bailey's wife, Susie, and Mitchell told her that she had gone too. Harriet thanked Mitchell for coming by and gave him money to buy grain for the farm's livestock.

As soon as Mitchell left, Harriet telephoned her husband in his Boston office. Micajah Clough then called Benjamin Johnson to share the news of Bailey's disappearance and took the next train back to Lynn. Arriving at about 3:00 p.m., he had his man put a horse on a team and started off with Harriet toward Breakheart Hill farm, dropping her off at Hannah Hawkes's house on the way. Best had heard Clough coming up the road and was already in the barn when he arrived.

"Where is George?" Clough asked as he drove into the barn.

"He has skipped and won't come back. This lady living with him was not his wife, it was his wife's half-sister. He had a wife and six children at Wiscasset, Maine, and he had an elopement when he came to Saugus four years ago and they didn't know where he was, and there was a reward offered and a warrant for his arrest."

Astonished, Clough asked, "How do you know this?"

"I told him about the reward. Here is a letter from Susie. As you can see, it's from Wiscasset, Maine."

Clough asked Best to get the keys and come with him to the camp. On the way, Clough asked Best, "Why didn't you notify the principals of his disappearance?"

"I was afraid he might come back. I was working on shares on the farm, not on the milk or eggs, but on the vegetables. That George played a mighty mean trick on me, clearing out in this way. George is a salesman and didn't allow me to do anything. He had about $90 he collected. I asked him on the Monday before he disappeared for $5 and he only gave me $3."

"When did George disappear?"

"I don't know except that we were together Monday afternoon and he went off with the milk. I was tired and went upstairs and went to bed. When I got up in the morning, I found the horse in the stall. The horse was unharnessed, and everything was in the proper place. It looked as if George had got back."

As Clough unlocked the camp door, he told Best that he could smell alcohol on his breath. Best said that he had bought a pint of whiskey and had been drinking it when Clough arrived and added, "What could a fellow do if a man used him as mean as George had?"

Best complained that Bailey hadn't attended to the produce business and that there were plenty of vegetables to sell, but they hadn't been sold as promptly as they ought to. He added that he didn't have any money to buy

Breakheart Hill camp, located a few hundred feet north of the farmhouse, shown here in 1942. *MDC photograph, DCR Archives.*

grain for the cattle. Clough thought a moment and replied, "I would like to have you—I will employ you. I will see that you are paid. This is quite a responsible position here with George gone. If you will keep out of drinking, keep sober, because we have got a good deal here, and we want a good man here, I will employ you."

Clough looked around the cabin and saw that one of the pictures had blown down and some water had collected around the hearth from that week's heavy rain. Clough showed Best where the leak was and said he would send a man from Lynn to make repairs.

Clough returned to Lynn with Harriet, hoping that he had resolved the farm's problems.[105]

Friday, October 12

James Thomas showed up at the farm again on Friday morning. Best asked him to come back at about 6:00 p.m. and join him on his milk run. When Thomas returned, he found Best in the barn. He had milked the cows and hitched a horse to the democrat wagon. Before leaving for Deary's farm, Best led Thomas into Bailey's bedroom and showed him a silver watch. "Where did you get it?" asked Thomas.

"Among Bailey's clothes."

"You had better put it back. I would not have it on me if I was you."[106]

After making the milk run and dropping Thomas off, Best drove to Lynn and stopped at a bar for a quart of whiskey before driving to Thomas O'Connor's blacksmith shop to get his horse shod. He had finished half of the bottle by the time he arrived at the shop. O'Connor was about to go to bed, but he agreed to do the job. As his fire had gone out, instead of a new shoe, he put an old shoe on the horse and put some nails in the other shoes.

O'Connor asked Best why he did not come in the daytime. Best replied, "I don't like to drive a horse barefooted." Then he added in a joking tone, "The police are bad fellows to get after you, and I don't want a horse without a shoe." O'Connor said the charge was twenty-five cents, but Best gave him twice that, saying that it was none too much, as he had got him out of bed. Best bade O'Connor a goodnight and drove back to Saugus in good spirits.[107]

Saturday, October 13

On Saturday afternoon, attorney Benjamin Johnson took a streetcar from Lynn to Howlett's Mill in Saugus. From there, he walked along the old highway through Breakheart Hill forest to the farm. He stood in front of the barn for a few minutes and heard the clatter of dishes in the kitchen. A moment later, John Best came out of the back door. Johnson, hungry after his trip, asked Best to go down to the orchard and get him a couple of apples.

While Best was in the orchard, Johnson went into the house and quickly looked around the ground floor of the farmhouse. Hearing Best return, he went out the back door and asked, "Where do you suppose Bailey has gone?"

"I think he has left the farm for good."

"Why do you suppose Bailey has gone without giving us any notice?"

"Bailey was a God-damn bad man."

"What do you mean by that? Why do you say that?"

"There are some things I know that I can tell if I have to, but I can't tell you now."

Annoyed at Best's tone of voice, Johnson said, "You ought not to take that position with me. You know that I am one of the owners of the place and you are a hired man and Bailey has gone. I have a right to know what you know about it. Mr. Clough has told me about this woman, Susie Young, not being Mr. Bailey's wife. That is a complete surprise to me as I had always supposed she was his wife, and if you know anything else that you can tell us, you ought to."

"I am not a hired man," Best replied. "I'm running the farm on shares with Bailey. I told Bailey that I should get my pay. I told him that 'these men who own the farm aren't skins like you and they will see me paid.'"

"I should hardly have thought Bailey would let you speak to him that way."

"Well, he didn't like it."

"I went to Mr. Deary's last night to see if I could learn anything about Bailey and he told me that Bailey was there Monday night with his milk as usual and that he owed Bailey some money, and offered to go upstairs and see his wife, who had the purse, and get the money for him. Now, how can you explain Bailey's going away that night and, at the same time, refusing to accept the money that Deary owed him?"

"Well, the officers were after him."

"What officers?"

"Maine officers."

"Well, how did Bailey know about these officers?"

"I told him. I told him Monday night."

"And how did you know that Susie Young was not Mrs. Bailey?"

"She told me."

"How came she to tell you that she was not Bailey's wife? Were there any improper relations between you and her?"

"No, there were not. She asked my advice about some things. She told me that she was not Bailey's wife, that she was going down into Maine and asked me if I thought it was well for her to take the boy with her."

The conversation was interrupted as Johnnie Mitchell drove up in a wagon leading one of the horses that Best had loaned him earlier that day. Johnson left the two men to put the horse away and feed the livestock and started walking back along the old highway to return to Lynn.[108]

Sunday, October 14

On Sunday morning, Clough returned to Breakheart Hill farm. As he arrived, he saw Best and Rowe in front of the barn. Clough asked Best if he had heard anything from Bailey. When Best said he hadn't, Clough said that he wanted to go through the house, which he had not entered for three years. He went from room to room and returned to the kitchen. There, he saw a rifle in a canvas case hanging on the wall. He told Best that it was a poor place to keep it because of the dampness of the wall and suggested that he put it behind the stove. Upstairs, Clough noticed that the scuttle access to the attic was partly open with a bucket under it to catch water. He made a note to himself to have someone come up and repair the leaks in the roof.

Clough then asked Best to bring him the keys to Breakheart Hill camp and to meet him there. Meanwhile, he asked Rowe to go into the forest with him to collect some plants for a fernery that he was creating. When Clough and Winnie reached the camp, Best was standing on the front porch with the burglar alarm ringing. Surprised that Best had been unable to unlock the door, Clough took the keys and showed him how to do it. He left the plants inside the camp, intending to return soon to plant them, walked back to the barn and drove away.[109]

Monday, October 15

After breakfast, Best wrote a note to Susie:

> *Friend Sussie Yours at hand, In due Season pleased to hear from you George has gone from hear* [sic] *wish if you have Seen him or have heard from him to let me know Some way Well say the Same as I heard you before or you Can Send a letter to Saugus. Will tell you more when I hear from you Yours truly, J.C. Best.*[110]

As he was folding the note and putting it in an envelope, there was a knock on the front door. Frank Philbrook, a carpenter from the nearby town of Malden, wanted to know if Best had any apples for sale.

"Who sent you?" Best asked.

"Mr. Griffin."

"Well, I'm milking right now. If you can wait half a minute, I will show you the apples."

A few minutes later, Best reappeared and led the carpenter out back to the piles of apples and asked, "What will you give?"

"Six cents a bushel for the cider apples."

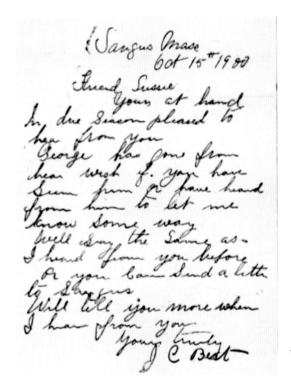

John Best's letter to Susie Young. From the *Boston Globe*, October 19, 1900. *Boston Public Library.*

"Well, my partner has disappeared and I don't know as I have a right to sell them, but I've talked with several people and they told me that I have a right." Philbrook said he'd be back the next day to pick up the apples.[111]

Tuesday, October 16

On Tuesday morning, Frank Philbrook returned to Breakheart farm with a wagon. He first loaded cider apples from the pile behind the house and then went down to the orchard to pick up more. Looking up, he saw a police wagon pull up to the farmhouse.

Charles Thompson was driving the horses, accompanied by three women, including his wife, Etta. Best appeared at the back door of the farmhouse. "Do you know where Mr. Bailey is?" Thompson asked.

"I think he is down in Maine. Who are you?"

"I am the police chief of Saugus. What is your name?"

"John C. Best."

"Could you give me Miss Young's address in Maine?"

"Box 174, Wiscasset, Maine."

"I want to write to her to see if she knows anything about Mr. Bailey."

Best pulled Susie's October 4 letter from his pocket and gave it to Thompson. While Thompson was reading, Best said, "I ain't so big a damned fool as people think I am."

He then told Thompson that the dogs had acted strange the day before. He started toward the orchard and shouted for Philbrook to come up. When Philbrook reached the farm, Best said, "Tell the gentleman how the dogs acted in the woods yesterday. Tell it to him."

Philbrook, who had no idea why he was being asked this, replied, "I was up in the woods the day before and the dogs acted as though they smelled something. They ran around and looked up in the trees."

Best thanked him and told him that he could go back to picking up apples.

Thompson asked Best to get the dogs so that he could observe them. A few minutes later, Best returned with two dogs, and the two men went into the woods. "We're liable to find Bailey's body hanging in a tree," Best said. But the dogs just calmly sniffed around the edge of the path.

When Best and Thompson returned from the woods, Etta and her friends were eating apples.

"Where did you get those apples?" Thompson asked.

Etta laughed, "We stole them."

Playing along with the joke, Thompson replied, "You are liable to get arrested."

In a quiet voice, Best interjected, "That is what I am afraid of."

Thompson shot Best a quick, curious look before getting into the wagon with the women and driving home.[112]

That afternoon, Clough drove to Breakheart Hill farm with his two partners, Benjamin Johnson and John Bartlett, and a man named Mr. Carpenter. When they arrived, Clough gave Best some sausages and steak in case he was short of food and introduced Carpenter, saying, "I brought him down here to look around the place, with the idea some time of coming here to take it."

Best said nothing but was surprised to learn that someone else was being considered for the caretaker job. Clough, Best and Carpenter walked to the farmhouse, and Best unlocked the door. Clough noticed that Best had been drinking. As they walked into the house, Best stepped away from him, prompting Clough to say, "Johnnie, there is no need of your keeping away from me. If you were fifty feet away, I could smell your breath. You promised me you wouldn't drink anything."

"My God, I promised I wouldn't get drunk. I didn't promise I wouldn't drink anything. I have got my own whiskey; I haven't got yours. I don't care if you have got more money than I have and if you were Willie K. Vanderbilt, it wouldn't make any difference."

After showing Carpenter around, Clough took him to the Saugus station to catch a train to Boston. Returning to the farm, he took Best aside and said, "I got a request that I would like you to comply with. I would like to have you sleep in George Bailey's room and that will give you just that part of the house, and I could take the two front rooms downstairs and upstairs and have them thoroughly cleansed."

"I will not sleep in that room for $500. I am afraid that George will come back and kill me. You don't know what a revengeful man—what a violent temper he has. Mr. Clough, I am scared, and I don't want to stay in the house alone anyway."

Clough urged Best to get Rowe or someone to come over regularly and help run the farm. If he did that, Clough said he would pay for crops that they brought into the barn, which would otherwise freeze in the fields. Clough left Best and walked back to the barn, where Bartlett and Johnson were waiting, and the three farm owners drove back to Lynn.[113]

5

GHASTLY FIND

Floating Bridge crossed Floating Bridge Pond in eastern Lynn on the old Boston-to-Salem turnpike. Although this road, Western Avenue, has a constant flow of traffic today, in 1900, the bridge was crossed mostly by farm wagons, livestock, carriages and pedestrians and was a lonely place after dark. For most of its five-hundred-foot length, Floating Bridge was almost level with the water, which was brown and opaque, evoking mystery. The bottom was so muddy and soft that no other type of bridge could be built, leading many to believe that the pond was bottomless.[114]

Approaching the bridge from the south, two houses were visible. At the far end of the bridge, there was a modest dwelling set back from the right side of the road. Across from this was the wooded approach to the Fay estate, its native forest mixed with foreign trees brought in by a former owner. At the near end of the bridge, there was a house on the right side facing a small restaurant.

The morning of Wednesday, October 17, 1900, was sunny and cool, with a brisk wind blowing from the northwest. James English, a gardener, and Fred Torrence, a grocery clerk, spent the early morning on the Fay estate collecting beechnuts. At about 10:00 a.m., they were heading back to Lynn across the bridge when one of them noticed something large in the water to their right, on the western side of the bridge. A closer look revealed a large burlap bag. Thinking that it might contain an animal, Torrence took his knife from his pocket and sliced through the coarse threads, exposing a black-and-white striped shirt, an undershirt and part of a suspender. As he

Floating Bridge over Floating Bridge (or Glenmere or Collins) Pond in Lynn. Built about 1804 as part of the Boston-to-Salem turnpike, this bridge was the first of its kind in the United States. On October 9, 1900, George Bailey's body was dumped, in five burlap bags, off this bridge. *Lynn Museum and Historical Society.*

cut deeper, they saw what looked like human skin. Horrified, the men ran along Western Avenue toward Lynn to find someone. They stopped at a barbershop several hundred yards from the bridge and told the owner, Frank Hunt, what they had seen.

"There's something funny about it," English said. "Come down and look at it."

"Oh, it's probably nothing but a dead dog," Hunt replied.

The two men insisted until Hunt agreed to accompany them to the bridge. Grabbing the floating burlap bag, they tried unsuccessfully to haul it out of the water. They released the bag, and English and Torrence set off to find a policeman.

A block past Hunt's store, they came across Officer Daniel Flynn. The three of them returned to the bridge, where Officer Flynn poked at the bag for a few minutes before saying, "There's something in that bag and I think it's a human body."[115] At that moment, a cart from the Lynn Ice Company happened to be crossing the bridge. Flynn waved for it to stop

Left: Lynn police officer Daniel Flynn. Published in 1895 in *Our Police* by Henry Fenno. *Lynn Public Library.*

Below: Patrol wagon that was probably used on October 17, 1900, to carry Bailey's remains from Floating Bridge Pond to Haven's undertaker rooms in Lynn. Published in 1895 in *Our Police* by Henry Fenno. *Lynn Public Library.*

and asked the iceman for his tongs. As Flynn recalled, "I took and stuck the tongs in the bag…and brought it up to where the middle rail and plank that runs close to the bottom of the bridge was broken out. I took one of the tongs and gave the other one to the driver of the wagon, Mr. Wells, and I lifted it on the bridge."[116]

As they lifted it, blood oozed out and spread over the surface of the water. The bag continued to ooze as it dropped with a thud onto the bridge. It was a ghastly sight. They could see clothing, a torn suspender and white flesh, which Officer Flynn briefly touched, finding it cold and very smooth.

He took out his knife and cut a half-foot-long slit in the bag, enough to reveal that it contained the headless torso of a man with his legs cut off about halfway between the knee and the hip. The bag also contained a large object, which later proved to be a rock.

Flynn ran to a police call box and telephoned Lynn police headquarters to ask for a patrol wagon, which doubled as an ambulance. The horse-drawn wagon arrived with Officers Herbert Morse and Thomas Murphy and a local newspaper reporter, Harlan Cummings.

Together, they loaded the dripping mess into the wagon, and Officer Flynn ordered them to take it to Michael P. Haven's undertaking rooms on Central Avenue in Lynn and to notify the medical examiner, Dr. Joseph Pinkham.[117] Cummings rode in the patrol wagon with the officers, showing the close relationship that then existed between the press and the police. That evening, Cummings's account, titled "Ghastly Find," was published in the *Lynn Daily Evening Item*:

> *The ghastly murder was disclosed this morning at Floating Bridge….*
> *The body of the murdered man, which cries out more eloquently for justice than if the tongue could speak, is a horrible ghastly sight, almost always to be covered over with the veil of silence, except in so far as it is necessary to aid in bringing the perpetrators of the awful deed to the bar of justice. The work was done by some person unfamiliar with anatomy, and in a bungling manner….*
>
> *The police are actively at work on the case although they are working on a blind trail. The supposition that the body was brought from out of town has prompted the police to communicate with the out-of-town authorities, and an examination of all the missing men cases….A systematic effort to find the remainder of the body is to be undertaken immediately.*[118]

Soon after the body arrived at his undertaking rooms, Michael Haven examined it and discovered that the man had been shot twice in the chest. His watch pocket contained an empty chamois bag. The watch had apparently been snatched away, as there were still a few links of the watch chain attached to a buttonhole. Another pocket contained two ten-cent pieces, three copper pennies and a small piece of hard rubber. One of the pennies, dated 1843, had a hole bored through it. His hip pocket contained several sheets of sodden paper. He was wearing a black shirt with a white stripe and a blue silk necktie marked "Rufus Waterhouse & Co., New York. Sold by the Harvard Co-operative Association, Cambridge."[119]

News of a murdered man found in Floating Bridge Pond traveled fast to local authorities and newsrooms. A *Boston Globe* reporter who was aware that George Bailey was missing rushed in his horse and carriage from Lynn to Breakheart Hill farm, arriving about noon. John Best opened the kitchen door and the reporter asked, "Has Bailey returned?"

"No, he has not."

"Can you describe what he was wearing when you last saw him?"

"Keep me out of this, for God's sake. I don't want my name mixed up with the disappearance of Bailey. As far as I know he won't come back. He left a wife and six children at Wiscasset, Maine, when he came to Saugus four years ago and there was a warrant for his arrest, so he skipped."

The reporter noticed a rifle hanging on the wall and asked Best what he used the gun for.

"I've had that gun to protect myself as I'm afraid of Bailey."

Taking his leave, the reporter drove his horse and carriage to the Saugus police station and told Chief Thompson about his meeting with Best.[120]

After the reporter left, Thompson called Officer Herbert Morse at the Lynn Police Department and asked him to accompany him to Breakheart Hill farm. When Best came to the door, Thompson said, "I'd like to go into Bailey's room to see if any of his clothes are missing." Thompson and Morse went through the sitting room and into the bedroom. They looked at the hooks behind the door and found an old shirt and some clothing. Morse said that the shirt was the same kind that had been found on the body.

Best asked, "What body?"

"A body of a boy that was found."

They went into the kitchen, and Thompson's attention was drawn to a rifle in a case standing in the corner behind the door. He picked it up and took it out of the case. Opening the chamber, he saw that it was dirty and had been shot recently. He asked Best, "Why do you keep a rifle there for?"

"I think Bailey is trying to undermine me."

"You better take a club of wood and knock him down, than to use a rifle on him."

Thompson put the rifle back into the case, returned it to the corner and asked Morse to ride with him to Lynn.[121]

While Thompson and Morse were questioning Best at Breakheart Hill farm, the medical examiner, Dr. Joseph Pinkham, arrived at Haven's undertaking rooms. After taking a cursory look at the torso and the torn burlap bag that had contained it, Pinkham telephoned his associate, Dr. Herbert Newhall, and asked him to help with the autopsy.

That afternoon, Pinkham and Newhall began the gruesome task of examining the torso. Also present were another physician and a reporter for the *Boston Herald*. The next morning, October 18, the *Herald* published this account:

> There is no doubt, in the opinion of the medical examiner, that the body was chopped almost immediately after the victim was murdered, and that a knife was first used to make an incision, and that afterward an axe was employed to sever the bones. It was a clear case of butchery. The bones at the ends of the several dismembered parts were crushed, the flesh was jagged, and it was the coroner's opinion that the axe was a dull one.
>
> The body was chopped to pieces while the clothes covered the victim. This is shown by the fact that the clothing is cut to correspond with the mutilation of the body. The front of the shirt is hacked in more than a dozen places, and the trousers reveal the same condition. The two bullets entered the victim's right breast. In the opinion of the coroner the first did not kill, and the second bullet was discharged while the victim was falling. The first bullet pierced the tissue in the back and was not found in the autopsy. The second bullet struck the breastbone and glanced off, lodging in the left side, where it was subsequently found. That shot caused instant death. Dr. Pinkham stated that it was his opinion that the body had been in the water eight to ten days, more or less.[122]

While Pinkham and Newhall were performing the autopsy, city marshal Thomas Burckes sent Officers Daniel Flynn, Edward Smith, Thomas McKenney and Charles Colby to Floating Bridge Pond to search for the rest of the body. Burckes was an athletic and muscular man with steely blue eyes. He had a reputation for being tough and liked to remind people that, while serving in the navy during the Civil War, he had survived for five days at sea without food or water.[123] The officers hitched a horse to a police wagon and drove to the pond. Finding no rowboats on shore, they drove to nearby Flax Pond and commandeered two boats from fishermen. They also took several long, hooked poles from a nearby icehouse. Flynn and Smith launched one boat from the northern side of the bridge, where the torso had been found, while McKenney and Colby launched the second boat from the southern side. Within minutes, Smith had pulled up a burlap bag. He sliced through the burlap with his pocketknife and saw that it contained a man's leg. Rowing back to shore, he tossed the bag into the patrol wagon and covered it with cloth.

Scenes at Floating Bridge Pond on October 17, 1900. Drawn by newspaper artist Dwight Case Sturges. From the *Boston Globe*, October 18, 1900. *Boston Public Library.*

A few minutes later, McKenney felt his hook catch on a large object on the south side of the bridge. Officer Colby helped him pull the bag off the hook and onto the bridge. The bag was marked "I.H. Estes" and was tied with a string. Looking inside, McKenney and Colby saw that it contained a man's right leg with trousers, stockings, a shoe and a rock.[124]

As dusk approached, Officer Morse arrived in a patrol wagon. Ignoring the growing crowd of onlookers, he and Officer McKenney put the two burlap bags into the wagon and drove back to Haven's undertaking rooms. Meanwhile, Officers Flynn, Smith and Colby rowed the two boats to the icehouse and hauled them inside for their use throughout the investigation.[125]

THE ARREST

S tate officer George Neal was at Salem Superior Court when he learned that the police had found a body in Floating Bridge Pond. Neal, a Civil War veteran and former Lynn city marshal, caught a train to Lynn. He walked to Haven's undertaker rooms to view the body and, suspecting that it was the missing man, Bailey, went to the police station to see city marshal Burckes. Officer John Bannon of Saugus, who had also seen the body, had already visited Burckes and told him that the clothes were like those he had seen Bailey wear on his milk runs.

Burckes asked Sergeant John Fitzgerald and Deputy Marshal David Bartlett to go with Officer Neal to Breakheart Hill farm but to wear civilian clothes. Neal asked Burckes if they had found any evidence that might be useful to take with them. Burckes handed him an evidence bag with straw needles that was found on the torso.[126]

As the men pulled the horse-drawn carriage into the yard between the barn and farmhouse, they noticed a light shining from an upstairs window. The officers walked to the front of the house, and Neal called out, "Halloa."

"All right, I'm coming right down!" Best said.

A moment later, he opened the door, and the officers entered. Neal asked, "Who are you? Do you live on the farm?"

"I do."

"Have you seen George Bailey? Do you know where he is?"

"That's what I want to know," Best replied.

The officers entered the sitting room and, as soon as they sat down, started asking Best questions. How long have you worked here? Are you sure that

State police officer George Neal. Published in 1895 in *Our Police* by Henry Fenno. *Lynn Public Library.*

you don't know where Bailey is? How long has he been missing? Where did you see him last? Best told the story he had told others—that he lived on the farm with Bailey and was entitled to the profits from half of the crops sold. Regarding the day that Bailey went missing, Best said, "On the day Mr. Bailey went away, he was down on the marsh all day and came home at night with a load of hay. We ate supper together—some meat and bread and corn—and, afterwards, Mr. Bailey got ready to carry his milk down to Mr. Deary's and that was the last that I saw of him when he went off with his milk—I have not seen him since."

Officer Neal said that they wanted to look around and signaled to the others to follow him into the kitchen. With the light of a kerosene lantern, Fitzgerald saw the rifle resting upright behind the kitchen stove. He went over to examine it. Best said that the rifle belonged to the farm's owners and that they always kept it on the farm. "What kind of a rifle is it? How does it work?" Fitzgerald asked. From Best's response, Fitzgerald gathered that he didn't know much about the gun. The officer cocked it two or three times before putting it back and asked, "Where are the cartridges?"

"They are in the cupboard in the other room," Best replied.

He brought Fitzgerald a box of cartridges, which Fitzgerald put in his pocket to take back to the station.

Next, the officers went into Bailey's room and found a striped shirt hanging on a hook and noted that it was similar to the one found on the murdered man's body. They also saw several pairs of worn and narrow size-ten shoes, the same size as the shoe found on the severed leg.[127]

They then climbed upstairs to Best's room. A bicycle was leaning against a wall, and the bed was unmade and strewn with clothes. A book lay on top of a box beside the bed. Opening the box, they found a half-empty pint bottle of whiskey. The officers also observed a large dark stain on the carpet. Similar spots were on the wall below the window and on the sill. It looked as if something wet on the floor had been picked up and thrown through the window. As described in the *Boston Herald*, "The wall underneath the window sill of Best's room was saturated with blood, and so was the carpet on the floor, and there was blood upon the window sill, and also some blood on the exterior of the house."

"This looks like blood," said officer Neal to Best. "It does look like it," Best replied. "I don't know how that came here. It was here when I came here five months ago. Some one might have had a nose bleed. I don't know anything about it." On the way downstairs, Neal continued asking Best questions.

"When did you last go to Lynn?"

"I haven't been there for a week, not since October 8."

"Did you have anything to drink that day?"

"Yes."

"Where did you get it?"

"George brought home a bottle of rum and I had drinks from that."

The officers began to question Best about Susie Young. At the mention of her name, Best took a letter from his shirt pocket and invited them to read it. Neal remarked that the contents seemed to indicate something more than friendship. "Well," said Best, "I am not saying anything, you can draw your own conclusion." As he said this, Neal caught an odor of alcohol on his breath.

They went out to look around the barn. Everything appeared to be in its proper place. Bailey's horse was in the stall, the wagon was in its place, the harness was hanging on one of several pins and the doors were closed. Best told them that he had replaced a broken wheel on the wagon when Bailey was there. And then, without prompting, he said, "I don't think George liked me because he thought I knew more than him."

On the way back to the farmhouse, Neal turned to Best and said, "Mr. Best, there has been a body found downtown and we would like to have you go down and look at it to see if it is Bailey's. You know Bailey better than anybody else around here, I think."

"All right, but the milk ought to go down to Deary's to-night. What is the matter with my taking a team and one of you fellows going with me with the milk to Deary's, and then I go down to Lynn?"

"All right. Where is your team? Where is your horse?"

"The horse is in the barn, but they are not shod all round. There is a horse down in the field that is all right."

Best started to walk rapidly down to the field. Suspecting that Best might be plotting an escape, Neal shouted for him to stop and said, "I guess you had better come back and take one of the horses in the stable."

"Well, they are not properly shod."

"Then let that milk go; you can carry that milk anytime."

"All right, but I have to go and shut those barn doors."

Best entered the barn through the cellar, followed by Neal. As they climbed the stairs, Best asked in a low tone, "Where was that body found?"

"Oh, up alongside the road, I guess," Neal replied.

Upon reaching the main floor of the barn, Best went into the grain room. Neal watched as he shoved his hands down into the barrel, down as far as his shoulder, and said, "I thought you were going to shut those barn doors. What are you hunting there for? What are you doing there?"

"I am hunting for something."

Best raised himself from the barrel holding a pint bottle of whiskey. He put it in his pocket before they walked out of the barn. Best turned around and closed the barn doors. He then took the bottle from his pocket and removed the stopple. As Neal stood by, Best chugged down the entire bottle and placed it on a nearby sleigh seat before getting into the police carriage with the three officers.[128]

The officers drove with Best directly to Haven's undertaking rooms. About 9:30 p.m., city marshal Burckes, Officers Fitzgerald and Neal and Best walked toward a gloomy undertaking room that had only a dim light burning. They stopped in the outer room as the undertaker lit the gas in the back room, revealing a covered form laid out on a slab.

Best and the officers stood beside the form as the undertaker removed the covering. Best looked at the revolting limbless body without moving a muscle and with no change in the flush on his face.

"Is that Bailey's body?" one of the officers asked.

"I cannot tell," Best replied calmly, "but I might be able to remember the clothes."

One officer held up the black trousers with ragged edges where the axe had torn them while cutting the legs. Another held up the striped shirt with ragged cuts where the same weapon had ripped the cloth as the murderer hacked off the head and arms. Best looked them over, appearing to be undecided whether he had ever seen them before. He then turned to the officers and said placidly, "I should say those clothes belong to Bailey."[129]

Officer Neal asked Best to go with him to the Lynn police station. Once there, they went into city marshal Burckes's private room, where several officers asked Best questions. Neal finally said, "Mr. Best, we shall have to hold you until this matter is investigated."

Neal asked Best to stand up. Reaching into his pockets, Neal pulled out a book. Best quickly said, "Don't lose that; that is my account book." Neal handed the book to Burckes and asked him to have an officer lock Best in a jail cell in the basement of the station. Later that evening, Neal went to Best's cell to ask for his sister Nettie's name and address. He found Best wide awake with no indication that he had been drinking.[130]

After Neal left, a *Boston Herald* reporter asked to see the prisoner and gave this account:

> He was lying upon the mattress, getting ready for a night's sleep, when the reporter aroused him. He said he was 35 years old and single, and that he had a sister living at 9 Marianna Street. He was perfectly at ease, a fact he took occasion to refer. "Do I look like a guilty man?" he asked, as he drew big clouds of smoke from a pipe he was puffing. He then went on to assert his innocence. "I don't think they can prove me guilty," he said. "How about the blood in your room?" asked the reporter. "That looks bad, I'll admit," he said. "It might have been caused by a nose bleed, but, if it was, I don't know anything about it." He claims that Bailey abused his wife, and that he had often heard them quarrelling …
>
> There is always a motive for a crime of this character, and the police claim to have discovered what that motive is. It can be expressed in two words. A Woman.[131]

That day, unaware of the dramatic events unfolding 140 miles south of her, Susie Young sat at a desk in her parent's cottage in Maine and replied to Best's letter of October 15:

Mr. Best,

I got your letter today. Was please to hear from yow, but sorry to hear George gorm. I don't know where he is if I did I let yow know. I feel worred but please write and tell me all yow know abut. I wrot a letter to him and it came back. I wrot to your sister and did not get eney answer. If he can't be found I shall half to come up. If they eneything wrong let me know. I told Mr. Mitchell what I want dun and if I half to come I make thing all right with yow. Please write as soon as yow get this and tell me all.

Yours truly

Susie L. Young[132]

THE INVESTIGATION

The following morning, October 18, the Lynn Police Court held a hearing for John Best to decide whether there was enough evidence to hold him. Court sessions were held daily at the police headquarters on the second floor, "a roomy, well-lighted and finely ventilated apartment, well adapted for the use to which it is put."[133]

Judge John Berry took his seat on the bench in the crowded courtroom. A dozen prisoners charged with drunkenness were in the dock. Best sat at one end of the dock far removed from the others with jailer Thomas Twisden standing beside him. Best was dressed in the same clothing he had worn when taken from his home the night before: a dark calico shirt, black trousers and a dark coat and a vest with several holes. He sat very still, looking uninterested in the proceedings except when he heard another man's name called and the judge impose a fine for a simple offense.

Best's name was the last one called by Clerk Charles Leighton. He stood up without a tremor. "You are held on suspicion of the murder of George E. Bailey."

"Not guilty, sir," Best replied. City marshal Burckes asked the judge to hold the prisoner until the police could make further investigations.

Judge Berry consulted with Clerk Leighton, who said, "John H. Best, you are held until Saturday morning, without bail." Without a word, Best walked from the dock and almost fell down the iron stairs leading to the jail below. Twisden, who was escorting Best back to jail, caught him as he slipped.[134]

Scene at the Lynn Police Court during John Best's arraignment, with Judge Berry presiding. Best stands in the prisoner's docket at right. From the *Lynn Daily Evening Item*, October 20, 1900. *Lynn Public Library*.

Meanwhile, the police wasted no time looking for evidence. State officers George Neal and Daniel Hammond and Lynn police officers Charles Colby and John Fitzgerald drove to Breakheart Hill farm, where they met Saugus police chief Thompson. A small army of newspaper reporters was already there, along with hundreds of people who had arrived on bicycles, in carriages and on foot. Overnight, the small rural farm had taken on a carnival atmosphere. The officers set boundaries to hold the curiosity seekers at bay, allowing only the reporters to join them. They searched all of the buildings and the neighboring woods but failed to find anything.[135]

While the police were searching the farm, a *Boston Globe* reporter was on a train to Wiscasset, Maine. He hired a carriage to take him to Sarah and LeRoy Young's cottage south of town and knocked on the door. Susie stopped preparing dinner to answer the door. The reporter identified himself and asked if she knew the whereabouts of George Bailey. She told him that the last she knew he was living in Saugus, that she had written to him, but her letter had been returned, and that she was greatly worried.

He then broke the news to her of the terrible fate that had probably befallen Bailey. According to the reporter, "She did not shriek, nor scream, neither did she faint away, but for a minute she tried to keep back the tears but couldn't do it. She closed the door of the room where her mother was sick in bed and then for a few minutes gave vent to her grief."

When Susie had recovered enough to speak, she said, "I knew something must be wrong. I knew it. I knew it, and it was only a day or two ago I told mother that that man with the knife must have killed him."[136]

Back in Lynn, city marshal Burckes ordered Officer McKenney to search Floating Bridge Pond for the missing head and arms of the murdered man. McKenney asked Officers John Garney, John Lyons and Loring Burrill to join him. However, Garney and Lyons wanted to devise a better method than using ice poles to probe the soft, muddy pond bottom. In the station's basement, they found a five-foot length of iron gas pipe. They used wire to attach about a dozen cod hooks to the pipe. They then passed a rope through the pipe and tied the rope ends together to form a triangle. Where the rope joined, they tied another length of rope for an officer to hold while they dragged the apparatus across the pond bottom behind a rowboat.[137]

When they arrived at the pond, a large group of onlookers had already gathered. The number grew to hundreds as the afternoon wore on. They watched as officers carried the two rowboats out of the icehouse and set out on either side of the bridge. Officers Lyons and Garney, on the south side, were equipped with the new grappling tool, while Officers McKenney and Burrill, on the north side, carried an ice pole. Almost as soon as Garney put his tool in the water, he snagged something and signaled to Lyons to stop. Before long, they had pulled up a bicycle, a rubber tire, milk cans, an umbrella, fishing poles, wagon wheels and bags of dead kittens.

About an hour later, Garney noticed that his tool was sliding or bumping over something, which he first thought was a rock. This happened several times before he and Lyons decided to pull up the pipe tool. As they hauled it over the side of the boat, they saw that one of the cod hooks had snatched onto a "gunny" bag. Untying the bag and peering inside, they gasped as

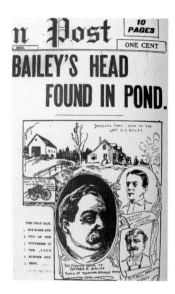

Boston Post headline on October 19, 1900. *Boston Public Library.*

a human head came into view. The bag also contained a rock that had been used to weigh it down. They signaled to the others, and the two boats met at the bridge. Burrill remained in his boat while McKenney took the dripping parcel from Garney and carried it to the patrol wagon parked beside the bridge.[138]

McKenney hopped back into a boat with Burrill to continue the search, this time with the grappling tool rather than the ice pole. About twelve feet from the railing, they snagged a feed bag labeled "I.H. Estes & Son, Hay and Grain, Lynn, Mass." McKenney opened the bag just enough to reveal two arms and a stone. As McKenney hauled the bag into the boat, something else dropped out and fell into the pond with a splash. "Something has dropped!" McKenny exclaimed, but they could only look on helplessly as the object sank to the bottom. One of the officers marked the spot with a pole before rowing to the bridge and taking the bag to the patrol wagon. Despite several later searches, the dropped object was never recovered.

The finding of the body parts created intense excitement among the crowd of onlookers that now thronged Floating Bridge. Those who had heard the rumor that the murdered man was Bailey pronounced in tones of certainty that it was indeed he. As the patrol wagon pulled out and headed for Haven's undertaking rooms, a stream of people followed in carriages and on bicycles and foot.[139]

At the morgue, a crowd at the entrance met the procession. Many of the men were workers who had stopped on their way home from their factory jobs. Women wept as men attempted to force their way through the doorway. Two officers jumped down from the patrol wagon and held the excited mob in check as the other officers took the frightful bundles inside.[140]

One of the people in the crowd was William Stiles, Best's brother-in-law. He identified himself to an officer, who cleared a passageway for him to enter the undertaking rooms. Upon viewing the body parts, Stiles almost fainted. When he had sufficiently recovered, he said to Haven and the officers standing about, "I should say that it is Bailey's head, but I could not swear to it, but the thumb I am sure is exactly as I remembered Bailey's injured hand."

Shortly after Stiles left, deputy city marshal Bartlett and Sergeant Fitzgerald went to Best's cell to bring him to Haven's undertaking rooms. Fitzgerald allowed Best to put on an overcoat before placing a "pair of twisters" on his wrist. As police led the suspect the short distance from the Lynn Police Court to Haven's, the crowd pressed around him. Best looked calmly from left to right, as if seeking a familiar face.

When the men entered the undertaking rooms, Fitzgerald passed his arm tightly under Best's to feel any tremor he might make as he faced the macabre scene. Haven opened the icebox that contained the head. There was a large bruise around the left eye and a smaller area of discoloration under the right eye. It was a horrible spectacle. The action of time and water, along with blows that the head had sustained, made it difficult to recognize the face.

Best walked to the back of the room with his head in the air, looking at the ceiling. He began to tremble, and Fitzgerald felt him shiver as he gazed nervously about the room, keeping the remains well below his line of sight. There was a pause as every man held his breath and waited for Best to speak. He was pale but kept his lips tightly together.

The sergeant looked at him and said, "That is Bailey, is it not?"

Best paused and let his eyes fall before calmly replying, "It looks like him."

"Ain't sure that it is him?"

"Yes," said Best slowly, "I am pretty sure that it is him, but I wouldn't want to swear to it."

"You have lived with him long enough to know what Bailey looked like, didn't you?"

"Yes, five months."

"Well, it's him," said the sergeant confidently.

"Yes, it's him, but I won't swear to it."[141]

Haven next brought out the bags containing the arms. Best looked at them and said he didn't know whether they were Bailey's or not. Fitzgerald asked Best if there was not a dislocated thumb on one of Bailey's hands, and Best said yes. The sergeant lifted one of the arms, showed the thumb to Best and asked him if that was not Bailey's. Best replied that he thought it was.

When Best emerged from the undertaking rooms, he was several shades paler than when he entered. Back in his cell below the Lynn police headquarters, he said he was tired and lay down. Later that evening, Officer Neal visited his cell. Best sat on the edge of his cot and answered questions with no attempt at evasion. He told Neal about his time working for Bailey and the quarrels between Bailey and Susie that led her to leave for Maine.

Looking up at Neal, he said that he thought Susie was afraid that Bailey's wife, Abbie, would come to Saugus and have her arrested.

"Did Bailey tell Miss Young that he did not have money to give her, and was tired of her?"

"He never said he was tired of her, but I heard him say that it would cost him a lot of money to get her ready to go away."

"Did she leave suddenly?"

"Yes, she was ready to go at any time, but she did not say the night before she went that she was going the next day."

Reaching into his pocket, Best produced a letter that he had received from Susie that afternoon, postmarked "Wiscasset, Maine, October 17." It was written with lead pencil and was more formal than her previous letters:

> *Mr. Best,*
> *I don't know where Bailey is. If he has gone away and there is any trouble there, I expect I'll have to go back. I have not seen him since I left. I am very sorry to put you to any trouble, but I wish you would let me know at once where he is. Your friend.*
> *Susan L. Young*[142]

The next day, October 19, several lawyers arrived at Lynn police headquarters, each claiming that Best had sent for him. Sergeant Fitzgerald, whose orders were to not allow anybody to see the prisoner, went down to Best's cell and asked if he intended to engage counsel. Best replied, "How can I engage counsel when I've only got $3?"[143]

That morning, Officer Neal and Chief Thompson went back to Breakheart Hill farm to continue to search for evidence. They spent several hours inside the farmhouse, barn and outbuildings. In the barn, they found a piece of rope, apparently cut with a knife from a clothesline and similar to the rope that had been used to tie the sack containing one of the victim's legs. They also discovered that a piece was missing from a long rope used to bind a haystack near the front of the barn. The ends of this rope also appeared to have been cut rather than broken from age or chafing.

While Neal and Thompson were doing their search, other officers were making the rounds of saloons where Best had bought liquor over the last two days to estimate how much money he had spent. The officers were struck by the fact that Best had flasks full of whiskey in both the farmhouse and barn while claiming to have little money. The bartenders confirmed that Best had visited their shops, but none had kept a record of his purchases.

Photograph of George Bailey's brothers. (*Left to right*): Benjamin, Charles Jr. and Henry Bailey. They came to Lynn on October 22, 1900, to transport Bailey's body back to Maine. *Courtesy of Mary Lou Bailey.*

The officers believed that Best had used Bailey's money to buy this liquor because Best had earned little from selling crops recently. The previous day, Hannah Hawkes, who lived just down the road from Breakheart Hill farm, had told investigators that Best told her that Bailey had given him only three dollars during the entire summer, much less than he felt entitled to receive. Also, she said that she had interceded when the tax collector tried to collect Best's poll tax and asked him to not press Best, as he had no money.

On Saturday, October 20, two of Bailey's brothers, Benjamin and Henry, arrived in Boston by boat from Portland, Maine, and took the train to Lynn. They waited at the train station to meet their brother Charles, who came on a train from Providence, Rhode Island. At about 7:00 a.m., the three arrived at the Lynn Police Court, where a crowd of several thousand people had already gathered. When the door opened at 9:00 a.m., there was a mad rush for seats. Henry and Benjamin Bailey secured seats, but Charles remained standing near the courtroom door. When all seats were taken, officers cleared everyone standing out of the courtroom, except Charles Bailey.

The prisoners marched into the courtroom, and Best sat in the dock, removed from the other prisoners. Attorney Linwood Pratt of Boston, who was hired by William Stiles to represent Best, walked over to the dock to consult with his client. Henry and Benjamin Bailey watched closely. Henry turned to the *Boston Globe* reporter sitting next to him and said, "Well, Best is cool. He's the coolest man I ever saw. And I believe he would actually be smoking a pipe if allowed to." Ben Bailey added, "Yes, he certainly takes things easy."

Judge Berry disposed of several cases, and the dock was cleared, except for Best. Court clerk Charles Leighton called Best, who stood up at once. He was dressed in a black calico shirt, a vest, trousers and a dark coat. Officer Neal presented the case for the commonwealth. Judge Berry asked if the defendant was represented by counsel, and attorney Pratt answered that he appeared for the prisoner. Neal read the arrest warrant: "George C. Neal, of Lynn, in the county of Essex, on behalf of the Commonwealth of Massachusetts, on oath complains that John C. Best, of said Lynn, on the 8th day of October, in the year of our Lord 1900, at Lynn aforesaid, and within the judicial district of said court, did assault and beat George E. Bailey, with intent to murder him, by shooting him or by some means, instruments and weapons to your complainants unknown, and by such assault did murder said George E. Bailey."

Officer Neal asked for a continuance of ten days, and attorney Pratt agreed, saying, "He is willing and anxious to have this mystery cleared up and the guilty man brought to justice. If by staying in jail ten more days he can assist in this he is willing to do so." Judge Berry ordered Best held until October 30 without bail and stated that he would soon schedule an inquest and that Best could assist the government by appearing as a witness. With every eye in the room riveted on him, Best calmly turned around and walked down the steps from the dock. Officers emptied the courtroom, but rather than disperse, most onlookers remained standing near the door or in nearby streets.[144]

After the court proceedings, Deputy Marshal David Bartlett and Officer Garney took Best in handcuffs to Carleton Shorey's photograph studio on Market Street for his police photograph. According to the *Lynn Daily Evening Item*, "Best posed without making any protest, and in contradistinction to the actions of many men whom the police have taken to be photographed, did nothing calculated to prevent the photographer from getting a good likeness. He faced the camera with a stoical indifference that marked him when he looked upon the severed head of the man he is suspected of having murdered." After this, Best was escorted back to his jail cell.[145]

Meanwhile, the three Bailey brothers hired a wagon to go to Breakheart Hill farm to see where George had lived and continued to Floating Bridge Pond to see where his body had been discarded. They then headed to Haven's undertaking rooms to arrange to take their brother's body home for burial in Maine. Once there, Charles Bailey was the only one with the courage to go inside. He insisted to the police that he wanted to make sure it was his brother before the family paid the expense of shipping the body back to Maine. He saw only the head, but that was enough. He later testified in court, "As I leaned over, I could see his moustache and the biggest part of the face."[146]

Charles Bailey assumed that he could act as administrator of his brother's estate and planned to ship George's personal effects to Wiscasset, where he would turn them over to Susie. However, officers at the Lynn police headquarters did not agree to his plan. In their view, Bailey's widow—Susie's half sister, Abbie—was legally entitled to his property. Losing this argument, the Bailey brothers left for Maine with George's body in a casket but without his personal possessions.[147]

At Breakheart Hill farm, the police had authorized Winnie Rowe to guard the property from the curious hordes but had done little to exclude them. It seemed that all roads now led to the Saugus farm. Local papers estimated that no fewer than five thousand people were visiting the scene of the Bailey murder daily. They came in carriages, on bicycles and on foot, and one curiosity seeker tried to travel the narrow road to the farm in an automobile. Chief Thompson of the Saugus police and his officers had only taken measures to prevent the crowd from accessing the house and barn, the locations most likely to contain evidence. Groups of spectators could be heard forming theories, which were met by counter theories, and so it went all day long.

Rowe was willing, even eager, to answer all questions. He told some strangers that he didn't believe that Bailey intended to visit his wife in Maine. He told others about the Saturday night before Bailey disappeared, when he and Bailey had come home together drunk from the neighboring gypsy camp.

Although the police had at first talked openly about the case, they had become more secretive and thought that the newspapers were shining too much light on their work and promoting too many speculative theories. On the morning of October 20, Sergeant Fitzgerald read in the Lynn paper that Rowe was telling people about a possible romantic relationship between Best and Susie. He decided to drive to the farm to ask Rowe what he knew.

Rowe told Fitzgerald, "I don't know whether Best was stuck on Susie Young or not, but I saw her sitting on his knee one day, just the same."

"What did you do when you saw that?" Fitzgerald asked.

"I laughed, and then, when Best came out of the house, I accused him of it, and he got very mad."

"What did he say to you?"

"He told me to shut up my head and called me a damned liar."

Fitzgerald made careful note of this conversation, as he regarded it as the most important so far—one that might help establish a motive for the crime.[148]

Meanwhile, Officer Neal decided that he wanted to speak with Susie in person and asked Officer Daniel Hammond, a former major in the Civil War who had worked with Hammond on several criminal cases, to go to Wiscasset to accompany her back on the train.

Hammond arrived in Wiscasset that Saturday afternoon, borrowed a horse and buggy from the local police station and rode out to the Youngs' cottage. Susie opened the door. After a hasty introduction, he told her that she needed to go with him to Lynn to help with the murder investigation and that the Lynn police department would pay for her travel, lodging and meals. Susie said she would go if she could stay at the home of Henry Mitchell, where she and Bailey had lived before moving to Breakheart Hill farm.

Early Monday morning, Susie met Hammond at the Wiscasset train station. She was neatly dressed in black with a heavy coat and new wide-brimmed felt hat. She brought a few articles in a small leather bag.

They boarded the 6:30 a.m. train and arrived in Lynn six hours later. After leaving the train, Officer Hammond accompanied Susie for lunch on Central Avenue before walking to the police station. There, after introductions, she climbed into a carriage with a group of police officers and drove to Breakheart Hill farm, followed by a contingent of newspaper reporters.

Above: Crowds of people visiting Breakheart Hill farm after Best's arrest. Drawn by newspaper artist Wallace Goldsmith. From the *Boston Herald*, October 25, 1900. *Boston Public Library.*

Right: On October 22, 1900, state officer Daniel Hammond accompanied Susie Young from Wiscasset, Maine, to Lynn. This sketch, by Harold Laskey, shows Hammond and Young leaving Bent's Restaurant on Central Street on their way to the Lynn police station. From the *Boston Globe*, October 23, 1900. *Boston Public Library.*

During the ride, Susie was cheerful and forthcoming. She answered every question quickly and directly, showing no desire to evade. She even answered questions that suggested that she had relations with Best, without denying that she had ever had "kindly feelings" for him. The officers were struck by the way she looked directly at them with her large, blue eyes. Her face and manner gave an impression of sincerity and truthfulness, and it was obvious that she felt affection for Bailey.

As the police and reporters traveled up the familiar road to the red farmhouse, they passed crowds of curious people. One newspaper later estimated that upward of ten thousand people had visited the scene that day. As they arrived at the top of Forest Street, tears began to roll down Susie's cheeks. She continued to weep as she stepped into the kitchen littered with pots and kettles, located exactly where they had been the night that Best was arrested.

Susie walked into the sitting room, which, unlike the kitchen, was in order. Looking over to the corner, she saw the crib where her baby had spent the days while she was doing housework, and she began to cry. Officer Hammond helped her to a chair, where she sat sobbing and swaying. "When I left here everything was pleasant," she said. "When I went away, I didn't expect to have to come back to such a terrible thing as this. George was kind to me, and we were very happy here. He never spoke an unkind word to me."

Once she had recovered, she accompanied the officers throughout the house. They returned to the kitchen, and she picked up the keys on the stove behind the kettle. "How often have I seen George with them," she said as she handled the brass chain with three keys—one to the lock on the kitchen door, one to the henhouse and a third to the tool house. "I don't believe they ever left him. When he changed his clothes coming in from work, he always transferred the keys from the pocket of one pair of trousers to the other. I don't believe anyone could have got these keys from Mr. Bailey before he was killed."

Looking around to the back of the stove, Susie picked up a small-handled hatchet and exclaimed, "Here is the hatchet we used to cut ice." Officer Neal took it from her and, upon examining it, observed dark red streaks on the handle near the eye and on the blade. Susie suddenly sobbed convulsively. "Oh, it's terrible. To think that George should have been murdered, and in such a shocking and brutal manner."

From the kitchen, they stepped into the storeroom, where old scraps of harness and corn husks were lying about. An officer pointed to some dark red stains on the wallpaper near the door. Susie said that none of the stains

SUSIE L. YOUNG'S VISIT TO THE BREAKHEART HILL FARMHOUSE.

Scenes of Susie Young's visit to Breakheart Hill farm on October 22, 1900, drawn by Harold Laskey. From the *Boston Globe*, October 23, 1900. *Boston Public Library.*

were there when she left for Maine. She scrutinized the floor and saw a large but faint blotch on the boards, about five feet long and two feet wide. "These marks were not there when I left the farm," she said. "I know this room, and I would have seen them. There was no break in the paper that showed the plastering like this. Someone has been scrubbing this floor lately. I don't understand it. It wasn't so when I went away." As she said this, she realized what might have happened in this room and began to cry. The officers glanced at each other, realizing that she had just provided support for their theory.

Officer Neal took out a saw and cut a piece of the stained boards from the floor and a piece from the door frame. He also took a section of stained wallpaper from the wall. He placed these, along with the hatchet from the kitchen, in a large basket. He would deliver these to Professor Wood at Harvard Medical School the next day to determine whether the stains were human blood.

After this, they went into Bailey's room, where Susie was unable to identify any missing clothing, except the corduroy jacket and black trousers that he was wearing when he was shot. They continued upstairs to Best's room, where Susie searched for the knife that she had often seen him carrying but could not find it.

Next, they went into the tool house, where Susie said Bailey kept two hatchets and four axes. They found all of these except one axe. Of the three axes, one was short-handled and had been sharpened recently. Susie described the fourth missing axe as a long-handled one and said it was dull and not fit for cutting wood.

Then they walked out to the barn. Officer Mansfield showed Susie a piece of burlap that had come from the bonfire that James Thomas, the neighboring farmer, had discovered still smoldering between the house and the barn the day after Bailey disappeared. Susie looked at it closely and said, "That is just like the burlap I used to line those red-striped horse blankets. There were two of these blankets, and Mr. Bailey always had one in the wagon, and the other was kept in the barn until cold weather."

When asked where they came from, she said, "I remember that Mr. Bailey brought them with him when he came with me from Maine to Henry Mitchell's. They were lined with burlap. I remember it because I lined them myself. They were worn out, but Mr. Bailey thought by lining them they would wear a little longer."

The officers turned to a different line of questioning. "Was there any jealousy on the part of Bailey because of Best?"

Susie opened her eyes wide and said emphatically, "No, there never was any reason why Bailey and Best ever should have any trouble on my account. They never did, and if Best killed Bailey, I am sure it must have been to get the money which Mr. Bailey had."

"You cannot recall any man, whether he worked for Bailey or not, who had any serious trouble with him."

"No, no one but Craig and Best."

Officer George Neal and police removing blood-stained boards from the farmhouse on October 22, 1900. (*Lower left*) Susie is comforted by George Bailey's brother Charles. (*Right*) Best's unkempt bedroom on the second floor. Drawn by Harold Laskey. From the *Boston Globe*, October 23, 1900. *Boston Public Library.*

Joseph Craig, one of Bailey's farmhands who had been cheated and threatened by him, was living in Lynn but had said nothing to the police for fear that they would attempt to connect him to Bailey's disappearance.[149]

On Tuesday, October 23, Officer Neal took the 8:30 a.m. train from Lynn to the Harvard Medical School in Boston to deliver to Professor Wood the articles that he believed were stained with human blood. The state's theory that Bailey had been cut up in the farmhouse storeroom

WORKING ON THE BAILEY MURDER MYSTERY.

Scenes of the police investigation in the Breakheart Hill barn, drawn by Harold Laskey. From the *Boston Globe*, October 24, 1900. *Boston Public Library.*

depended on the result of Dr. Wood's chemical analysis. If the stains were human blood, the officers believed it would be difficult for Best to explain how they came to be there.

Neal was hoping for a quick answer, but Dr. Wood had an appointment in Worcester that day. He told Neal that he would try to make a finding by Thursday, but based on his experience, he thought that the spattering on the wallpaper, door frame and hatchet was probably human blood.[150]

By this time, the investigation was following multiple leads. On October 24, state police captain Harry Proctor traveled to New Haven to consult with the manufacturer of the .38-caliber rifle that police had found in the Breakheart farmhouse. As well as the rifle, he brought a box of ammunition that they also found in the house and the two bullets removed from the dead body. Proctor wanted to know whether Bailey had been shot with a revolver or with the rifle. He was confident that an expert at the factory would be able to resolve this by examining the bullets.

The police theory was that Best had shot Bailey while he was sitting in his chair in the farmhouse sitting room. Susie had told them that Bailey was in the habit of sitting in his chair after a day's work and leaning forward with his elbows on his knees. The police believed that Best had stood in the doorway to the kitchen and fired the rifle, which would account for the downward angles that the bullets took before entering Bailey's chest.[151]

On the morning of October 25, the police received a letter from Oakes N. Palmer, a jeweler in Pittson, Maine, giving a description of Bailey's watch. The Maine jeweler, who had repaired the timepiece in 1891, said it was a size sixteen, seven-jewel, gold-filled, open-face Elgin watch. Bailey was always known to carry a gold watch, but it apparently had been stolen by the murderer. When his body was discovered, there was only a small portion of the chain, which caught on the vest, and a chamois cover made by Susie in the watch pocket of the trousers.[152]

By Friday, October 26, even without reports from the experts on the blood stains and bullets, the state police believed they had enough evidence to hold Best and were ready for the hearing scheduled for the following Tuesday. The officers thought it was unlikely that Best would take the stand and attempt to explain away the evidence, although mostly circumstantial, that the police were ready to present.

The state, represented by Officer Neal, was ready to claim that Bailey returned to Breakheart Hill farm after delivering milk to Charles Geary. His claim would be based on the fact that, when searching the farmhouse, police had found the coat that Bailey had worn when last seen alive, as well as keys that Susie said never left his possession.

Neal would also show that Best had the weapon, a rifle, that could have been used in the crime and that he had motives of robbery and revenge. Also, Best had admitted to quarrelling with Bailey before Bailey set off for Deary's farm. Even though Best had given few details of this quarrel, the police made it a central feature of their narrative. According to them, Best "had words" with Bailey and then brooded over this encounter and, being drunk, added a drinker's remembrance of past wrongs or supposed wrongs, leading him to shoot Bailey. This chain of events was, the police claimed, the culmination of an unsatisfactory life on the farm that Best could no longer endure.[153]

As they were developing this story, another discovery strengthened their case. On October 27, officers went to the Breakheart farmhouse, taking with them stones that were in the bags containing Bailey's remains. They examined the stone walls near the farmhouse and barn and found a place in a wall where several stones were missing. Except for these, the wall was "complete and very regular." They were able to fit the stones they had brought into the vacant spaces and determined that they resembled the other stones in the wall.[154]

On October 20, police moved Best from the jail in the Lynn police headquarters to the Salem jail. On October 27, one of Best's jailers told a *Boston Post* reporter that Best was "the most unconcerned prisoner" there and retained a calm demeanor, reading when alone and eating heartily when meals were brought to him.

The jailer also said that, other than his attorney, Best had received only one visitor, his brother-in-law, William Stiles. During the time he had spent in the Lynn and Salem jails, Best had taken no "alcoholic stimulant" and did not seem to desire it. When he went to Salem, his tobacco was taken away, but he had not asked for it since. He had received no letters, flowers or "food delicacies." The jailer described Best as "the same stoic the police found when they took him to identify the remains of the man he is accused of murdering" and "a remarkable prisoner, never showing by any word that he is willing to explain the things that might cause his release."[155]

On the morning of October 30, Officers Fitzgerald and Colby went to Salem jail, where they handcuffed Best to Fitzgerald and walked him to the train station and caught the 9:01 a.m. train to Lynn. At the Lynn depot, several hundred people had gathered to catch a glimpse of the prisoner. As Best stepped from the train, there was a rush to secure a place along the path where he and the officers would pass to get to the patrol wagon that would take them to the Lynn police headquarters.

In the wagon, Best complacently smoked a cigar and smiled as he said to the officers that he had expected a larger crowd. He spoke about the weather but did not mention the case, and the officers did not bring it up.

A crowd of about three hundred people met the patrol wagon when it arrived at police headquarters. Again, Best said that he thought there would be a larger crowd and that the officers must have fooled people by not giving out the time they were to arrive.

Best presented a far different appearance from when he had first stepped into the Lynn police headquarters on October 17. Now he was clean-shaven with neatly combed hair and a smile that played around his mouth. He wore a dark brown winter overcoat over a dark suit and white shirt and newly shined shoes. He had evidently gone to considerable trouble to strike a groomed appearance.

The officers placed Best in a temporary jail cell, gave him tobacco and allowed him to light his pipe. He sat smoking with evident pleasure until he was brought into court.

As Best entered the court, he smiled at the reporters and nodded to them pleasantly from the dock. Officer Neal addressed the court, "May it please the court the government has been industriously at work on this case, but they come here this morning unprepared to try this case at the present time. We would respectfully ask for a continuance until a week from Thursday."

Attorney James Sisk of Lynn stepped forward. He had recently been hired by William Stiles to help attorney Linwood Pratt defend Best. Sisk said that as the prosecution was not ready to present its case, he was not going to reveal Best's defense at this time. However, newspaper reporters were able to discover the defense strategy and presented it in their newspapers. Best would claim that he was ignorant of where Bailey went after his regular milk run to Deary's. He would then speculate that an unknown assailant shot Bailey and dumped his body in Floating Bridge Pond. Meanwhile, Best would assert that after doing chores, he enjoyed a quiet evening alone and went to bed early.

Sisk had no objection to a continuance and added, "I understand that in the meantime there will be an inquest and that the government will be ready to go on at that time." Judge Berry ordered a continuance until November 8, and Best walked from the dock to the jail below.[156]

On Thursday, November 1, Bailey's possessions were auctioned off at Henry Mitchell's farm, with the proceeds to go to his second wife, Abbie Bailey. The crowd that gathered at Mitchell's corner in North Saugus was typical of a county fair. Farmers came in all sorts of vehicles, including some on "the electrics." The crowd was good-natured and smiled and joked as poor Bailey's things were handled and discussed.

"Special Administrator" Eben Smith had been charged with selling all goods at whatever price could be obtained, with only cash accepted. He succeeded in selling most of Bailey's possessions, including Bailey's livestock, wagons and harnesses. There was considerable interest in his little black mare, but when auctioneer E.A. Tibbetts asked for a bid, only one person raised his hand at the starting bid of $10.00. The auctioneer encouraged others to bid higher, but bids stopped at only $16.00. The buyer then bought

Sketch showing parts of John Best's legal defense during his October 1900 arraignment. From the *Boston Post*, October 28, 1900. *Boston Public Library.*

the buggy for $1.25, the harness for $0.25 and the buggy robe for $0.10 and happily drove off in his new horse and buggy.

Two barrels of apples sold for $1.10, while a pile of old wheels and boxes brought $2.50. People were liberally helping themselves to the barreled apples, even as they were being sold. Worse still, while the auction was in progress, Henry Mitchell laid a pocketbook containing some valuable papers and a large sum of money on a bench, only to have it disappear.[157]

On Thursday, November 8, Best was brought to Lynn from his Salem jail cell by Officers Fitzgerald and Colby for the continuance of the inquest.

This time, he was not handcuffed. Still enjoying his newfound celebrity, he smoked and chatted pleasantly with the officers about the weather and the presidential election. In a rematch of the 1896 race, Republican president William McKinley had just defeated his Democratic challenger, William Jennings Bryan.

Best smiled as he entered police headquarters and bowed to the officers as he stepped into the dock. He looked with interest at the large number of spectators, many of whom had been standing around the courtroom for two hours for an opportunity to witness the proceedings.

During the hearing, Best sat with his overcoat on, at times leaning over the railing of the dock as witnesses, including the medical examiner, the officers who had found Bailey's body, his neighbors Hannah Hawkes and James Thomas and Breakheart property owner Benjamin Johnson recounted their stories and conversations with Best. As they testified, Best constantly chewed tobacco. He laughed heartily with the spectators when Winnie Rowe said that Best had once proposed that if he could not hoe cabbages faster than Bailey, he would allow Bailey to shoot him. He also smiled when seventy-eight-year-old Thomas took a memorandum book from his pocket to refresh his memory while he was testifying.

Everyone in the courtroom seemed to take the proceedings more seriously than Best, and when court adjourned for the night, he shook attorney Sisk's hand and laughed and conferred with him for a few minutes.[158]

The hearing resumed the next morning. The courtroom was crowded long before the hour set for the trial arrived, and many were unable to gain admittance. Best entered the dock shortly before 10:00 a.m., looking well after a good night's sleep in a cell at the police station. He continued to display his usual coolness, occasionally stroking his mustache and smiling at acquaintances. He was apparently the most unconcerned man in the courtroom, and many remarked on his wonderful nerve.

The testimony was generally against Best, yet he was stoical to the extreme. He listened silently as his friend Johnnie Mitchell testified about the days he had spent with Best following Bailey's disappearance and as Fred Burnell testified that he had noticed Best and Susie having some affectionate "smarty" words together when Bailey was absent.[159]

But the sensational news of the morning was the prosecution's decision to not present any evidence regarding the alleged bloodstains found around the farm. This led many reporters and spectators to conclude that investigators had failed to find any human blood and did not want to risk having the prisoner set free for lack of evidence.

Attorney Sisk, senior counsel for Best, stood up to ask that the government case be thrown out and that his client be discharged. Judge John Berry said that he would decide the next day whether or not to hold Best on the charge of murdering Bailey.

After the noon recess, state officer Neal took the stand and demonstrated how rapidly the rifle found in the house could be fired. Attorney Sisk objected to this exhibition, but the officer proceeded and showed the court that two shots could be fired in less than three seconds.[160]

The government was ready to close its case. At this point, Sisk made a serious error and "threw a bomb [actually a gift] into the prosecution camp" by calling state officer William Proctor as a witness. The government had not intended to have Proctor testify, but Sisk had called him. Proctor had taken the .38-caliber rifle from the Breakheart Hill farmhouse and to gun experts to determine whether the bullets found in Bailey's body were fired from this weapon or from a revolver. Proctor testified that the experts had done experiments on the grooves in the bullets that showed they had come from this rifle.

This shocking testimony was followed by a commotion in court and the sound of Best laughing heartily. One of the lawyers had taken a chair and tilted it back against the gate in the railing in front of the witness seats. The gate opened, throwing the lawyer to the floor. Best enjoyed this episode very much.[161]

The hearing continued through the morning of the following day, Saturday, November 10. Speaking for the prosecution, District Attorney Scott Peters pointed to Best and said, "There is the murderer."

Everyone in the courtroom looked at the prisoner. Best never flinched and kept chewing gum and smiling, not once lowering his eyes, leading Peters to say that his conduct was remarkable in the annals of crime. When Peters had concluded, Judge Berry said:

> *The case has been so fully discussed, there is but little to be said. A horrible murder has been committed by somebody. It has startled the whole community. There is no accident about it. A man has been murdered and cut up. It could not have been done on the highway. It must have been committed where the person who did it had the opportunity to cover up evidences. The man must have been murdered and cut up where there was little chance of being seen, such a place would be the farm. From all the evidence, this man got back to the farm, because Best said he heard him. Either he must have been murdered by this man, or someone else who came on the place....It is*

not my place to find Best guilty or innocent. I find by the evidence conflicting statements….I am satisfied that a team went away from the farm, and went back, and that is the end of the road. Therefore, upon the evidence and Best's conduct since the government started to investigate, I will hold Best for the action of the grand jury without bail.[162]

Two months later, Best was arraigned in Salem Superior Court and entered a plea of not guilty. Newspaper coverage turned to a larger, global story three days later, when, on January 23, 1901, Queen Victoria died on the Isle of Wight. Best was left to languish in the Salem jail until his trial in March. On February 23, a story buried in the inside pages of the *Boston Post* reported that Best had been deserted by all except his sister Nettie, her husband, William Stiles, and Best's counsel, James Sisk.

Nettie was convinced of her brother's innocence. She told anyone interested that he was always cheerful and laughing and was the last man in the world to do any act like that of which he was accused. Despite his lack of freedom or visitors, Best was reported to be "the same cool fellow" that he was when arrested, taking things as they came and never causing any trouble for his jailers.[163]

8

THE TRIAL

John Best's trial was set for March 1901 in the Salem Superior Courthouse on Federal Street. The last person tried in this court for a capital offense was Alfred Williams, who, in 1898, was found guilty of first-degree murder and hanged in the Salem jail yard, the last hanging to take place in Essex County. After that, convicted murderers were electrocuted in the state prison in Charlestown, near Boston.

Best was to be tried before Justices Edgar Sherman and Jabez Fox, with Attorney General Hosea Knowlton, District Attorney W. Scott Peters and Assistant District Attorney Roland Sherman representing the government, and James Sisk and Nathan Clarke representing the prisoner.[164]

Knowlton was best known for his role as chief prosecutor in the 1893 Lizzie Borden trial and his rare courtroom defeat in that case. At the time of Best's trial, Knowlton had tried more murder cases than any other Massachusetts lawyer and was becoming known as an ardent opponent of the death penalty.

On Monday, March 18, the first day of the trial, deputy sheriffs Timothy Crowley and Arthur Bishop brought Best in a closed carriage from the Salem jail to the Salem courthouse. Unlike the crowds at the Lynn courthouse the previous November, there were few spectators on Federal Street to view Best's trial because this day was to be devoted to impaneling the jury. On subsequent days, spectators could enter the court if there were available seats.

By 9:30 a.m., 106 potential jurors, as well as newspaper reporters, clerks, court officers and lawyers, had filled most seats in the courtroom. Three court reporters were on hand to record the proceedings under the direction of a court stenographer. Each was to take notes for a few minutes and then go into one of the jury rooms and dictate his notes to one of four women typewritists.

As Best entered the courtroom, all eyes were on him. Undeniably a good-looking man, he was clean-shaven, with his hair parted on the right side and carefully brushed smooth. He was neatly dressed in a dark suit, with a white shirt and cuffs and a blue tie and checked pants. Over his suit, he wore a blue double-breasted Prince Albert coat. He took his seat and began an earnest conversation with his counsel, James Sisk. He then looked around, calmly scanning every face in the room.[165]

Attorney General Hosea Knowlton, a prosecutor at John Best's trial. Knowlton became famous as chief prosecutor at Lizzie Borden's 1893 trial in New Bedford, Massachusetts. Photograph by J.E. Purdy of Boston. *Library of Congress.*

Attorney General Knowlton announced that John C. Best was charged with four counts of murder in the first degree: one for each bullet fired into George Bailey, one for killing him with an axe and one for killing him with an unknown weapon. District Attorney Peters stood and told the terrible story that the prosecution had developed based on circumstantial evidence. Best sat in his armchair listening intently, leaning first to one side and then to the other. He grasped the arm of his chair with one hand as Peters described how he allegedly chopped up the body of Bailey with a knife and an axe and attempted to dispose of it forever in the murky depths of Floating Bridge Pond.

When Peters had finished, Knowlton motioned for a jury to be selected and told Best that he had a right to challenge twenty-two potential jurors.[166] Best stood while the jurors were called. Each was asked: Are you related to the prisoner or to the deceased? Have you any interest in the cause or expressed any opinions in the case? Are you conscious of any bias? Have you such opinions as will preclude you from finding the prisoner guilty and punishable by death?

Best's junior counsel, Nathan Clarke, advised him when to challenge a juror. Each time, Best would say in a clear voice, "Challenge." His demeanor remained cool, as it had been since his arrest.

Jury for the Best trial and the police chaperones. (*Front row, left to right*): James Trask, John Lane (foreman) and Fred French. (*Middle row, left to right*): John McGrath, Warren Bennett and Edward Merrick. (*Back row, left to right*): Elmer Briggs (deputy sheriff), Charles Mears, Joseph Wilkins, Fred Libby, Charles Pickett, Edward Hodgkins, Thomas Hunter and Roger Howe (deputy sheriff). Photograph by Robb Studio, Salem. From the *Boston Morning Journal*, March 31, 1901. *Boston Public Library.*

Just after noon, roofer James Trask of Salem was accepted as the twelfth juror. In impaneling the jury, 80 names had been called out of the 106 on the list. Of these, 18 were challenged by the government, 19 by the defendant, and 31 were excused by the court. The selected jury included tradesmen from nine nearby towns.[167]

When the court reconvened in the afternoon, the jury chose John Lane of Amesbury, a carriage maker, to be the foreman. Knowlton made a motion for the jury to view the crime scenes, Breakheart Hill farm and Floating Bridge Pond, the following morning. With that, the jury left in carriages for their rooms in the Essex House Hotel in Salem, which the county was providing free of charge for the duration of the trial.

The next morning, March 19, there was snow on the ground. A chill, wintry wind was blowing as the jury members left their quarters in the Essex House accompanied by deputy sheriffs Elmer Briggs, P.F. Tierney and Roger Howe. The group attracted considerable attention as it marched down the street two-by-two to the train station. They boarded the 9:18 a.m. train for Lynn, where a covered carriage called a barge was waiting. District Attorney Peters, attorneys Sisk and Clarke and state officer Neal rode in a landau.

The procession began the five-mile trip to Breakheart Hill farm by way of Charles Deary's farm, where Bailey had delivered milk on the fateful night of October 8. As they approached Breakheart Hill farm, they saw cordwood

Police overturned George Bailey's old democrat wagon at Breakheart Hill farm during their search for blood stains. From the *Boston Journal*, October 19, 1900. *Boston Public Library.*

piled in long, regular rows, showing that somebody had been industriously at work on the place since Bailey had lived there.

The jurymen were free to roam about the Breakheart camp, barn and farmhouse, but by court instruction, only District Attorney Peters and attorney Sisk could speak to them and then only to point out places and things connected to the crime. Peters showed the jurymen an area of higher ground near the side of the barn, where the government now alleged that Best had fired the shots that killed George Bailey as he emerged from the barn cellar. They viewed Bailey's old democrat wagon and the wheel that Best had removed. They then entered the farmhouse.[168]

The house had undergone a great change since the new caretaker, Charles Cole, and his wife had moved in. When Bailey, Susie and Best had lived there, it had been unkempt and dirty. Now it was "neat and bright as a new pin." The walls in the storeroom off the kitchen that had been stained with what looked like human blood were now repapered. Of the furniture that had been in the house, only Bailey's favorite armchair remained. "Do you hesitate to sit in it?" a *Boston Post* reporter asked Mrs. Cole.

"Not at all," she answered brightly. "The associations of this house do not affect me or my husband at all."

Charles (or William or Henry) Cole and his wife. Cole became caretaker of Breakheart Hill farm in October 1900, after Best's arrest. Mrs. Cole is holding Julia, a white poodle that was Best's favorite pet. From the *Boston Morning Journal*, March 24, 1901. *Boston Public Library.*

The barn where Bailey was alleged to have been killed was now well kept, and the white poodle that had been Best's beloved pet wandered freely around the house and barn.[169]

Leaving Breakheart Hill farm, the jurors traveled to Floating Bridge Pond over the same route that state prosecutors believed Best had driven with Bailey's body on that rainy night five months earlier. The weather was bleak as the party passed the ancient Hawkes place, where Hannah Hawkes claimed to have heard a team passing and repassing on that fateful night. Turning left off Forest Street, the barge headed to the Newburyport Turnpike. The curtains of the barge only partially cut off the wind. The jurymen grew cold and wrapped themselves in horse blankets. Soon a yellow house, the home of a woman who claimed to have heard two shots fired in quick succession, came into view.

The procession made its way along the shores of Walden Pond in a section of Lynn called Lynn Woods. The road was covered with uneven amounts of snow, and the barge got stuck in a snowdrift. The jurymen reluctantly climbed out of the vehicle to lighten the load, and the four horses pulled it

Scenes of Best's trial and the jury's March 1901 visit to Breakheart Hill farm and Floating Bridge. Drawn by Dwight Sturges. From the *Boston Globe*, March 20, 1901. *Boston Public Library.*

from the deep snow. Strangely, they had stopped beside a rock on which the single word "REPENT" was painted in black letters. Why it was written there or whether it was there last October, nobody knew, but with Bailey's murder on their minds, for some it took on prophetic significance.[170]

Soon they entered a settled part of Lynn, and District Attorney Peters pointed out a house on Lake Street, where, on that October night, a person had seen a team pass in the light of an electric lamp. Near Floating Bridge, he noted another house where someone claimed to have heard the fall of horse's hoofs. Once on the bridge, the jurors peered over the railing where James English and Fred Torrence had discovered the burlap bag containing Bailey's torso.

The cold and hungry jury returned to Salem for the afternoon's court session. Best entered the courtroom at 3:20 p.m. Three times as many spectators as those present had been turned away after the room was filled. More than a third of the spectators were women.

As Best passed the press table, he smiled at the reporters. Madelaine Stuart, society columnist for the *Boston Post*, the only woman journalist covering the trial, wrote, "It seemed strange, very strange. You would think that the sudden hush as he enters and the concentrated gaze of hundreds of eyes would shake his composure, would keep his own eyes upon the floor to avoid those other curious, staring eyes. He avoids them without effort. He simply ignores them. Yes, this man's nerve is wonderful."[171]

The jury entered a few minutes later, followed by the court officer with the white rod. "The court!" he cried. Everybody, except Best, stood up as the justices and counsels filed in. "Hear ye, hear ye, hear ye!" called the court officer and bid those who had business with the bench to "draw near, give your attention and ye shall be heard. God save the Commonwealth of Massachusetts!"

The prosecutors laid out their case. On the night of October 8, 1900, after Bailey returned from delivering milk to Charles Deary, Best waited outside for Bailey to exit the barn through the cellar door and shot him twice in the chest with a .38-caliber Winchester rifle. He put the body on horse blankets from the barn and used an axe and large knife that he always carried with him to cut off Bailey's head, arms and legs. Next, he put the body parts and the axe in empty grain sacks and added rocks from the nearby stone wall to weigh down the bags.

Best loaded the bags into a democrat wagon and drove rapidly down Forest Street and along the Newburyport Turnpike to Floating Bridge Pond, where he dropped the bags over either side of the bridge. He then drove back to Breakheart farm and, the following morning, burned the horse blankets.[172]

Police officer John McKenney testified about how Bailey's body was found. Following this, state officer George Neal brought in the grain sacks, the rocks, the ropes and the clothing taken from the body and arranged them in full view of the jury. These grim objects lay as dumb witnesses to the crime, to its revolting details. The spectators could not keep their eyes from them, especially the heap of stained clothing. Some turned pale and shuddered, yet they still gazed and gazed.[173]

Best listened to the testimony of the police officers, medical examiner and undertaker about finding the body parts and their ghastly condition without a shudder or wince. He looked at the evidence strewn on the courtroom floor without a sign of sentiment.

Court reporters came and went every few minutes, relieving one another. The lawyers examined and cross-examined, consulted with one another and took notes, as did the dozen or so reporters. Artists made sketches. Newspapers had assigned their best artists to the trial. One of the most eminent was Dwight Case Sturges of the *Boston Globe*. At just age twenty-seven, he was one of the best "etchers" in the business.

For the next nine days, a series of witnesses testified, mostly for the prosecution. In all, the government called fifty-five witnesses to the stand. The courtroom was full every day, and those who couldn't get in gathered around the doors to see the prisoner as he passed on his way to his closed carriage. Crowds clamored for admission, pressing so hard against the great doors that the police resorted to placing a wooden brace against the doors to prevent them from being broken. Just before closing the doors completely, they would let a few more in through the crack, and another day would begin.

On Wednesday, March 20, 1901, the *Boston Post*'s Madelaine Stuart reported from the courtroom, which she described as "light, high-ceilinged, high-windowed, airy, almost cheerful":

> *Best fascinated me. He interested me much more than even the woman in black—Susie Young. He has a strange face; a face that seems capable of but three expressions. One seems to be habitual, a stolid, emotionless look. Another is a sardonic sneer in the form of a smile. The third is—I almost hesitate to say it, but I believe I am right—an expression of utter sadness.*
>
> *Susie Young—well, Susie Young's expressions are hard to fathom, for she is clothed in mourning for Bailey's death, and part of her garb is a thick veil, which allows only a faint glimpse at her very pale face. Enough is seen, however, to show that Susie Young has regular and quite pleasing features. Her bearing in the court room, where she is the object of so much curious gazing, is very quiet, almost dignified.*[174]

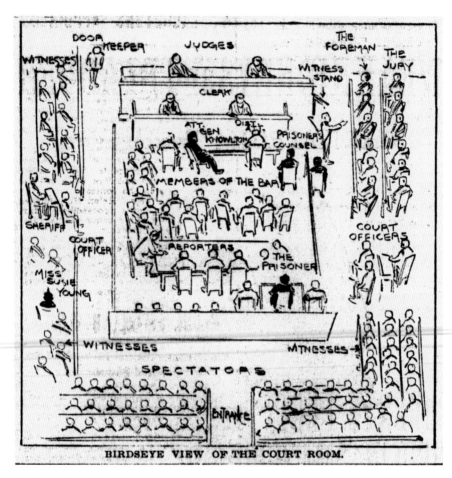

BIRDSEYE VIEW OF THE COURT ROOM.

Birds-eye view of the Salem courtroom, where John Best's trial was held. From the *Boston Post*, March 19, 1901. *Boston Public Library.*

On that day, among others, eighty-six-year-old Hannah Hawkes and her grand-niece, Henrietta, testified. Hannah presented a striking appearance. Dressed in black with a black bonnet on her head, she walked briskly up the aisle to be sworn in.

"You may have a chair to sit in, Miss Hawkes," Judge Sherman said.

"I guess I can stand. I thank you."

Hannah stood for nearly two hours and told about her life on Forest Street and what she knew of Best and Bailey and the peculiar rattling sound of Bailey's wagon as it approached her house each day. She said she saw Bailey drive by at about 8:00 p.m. on the evening of October 8 and recognized the sound of his wagon between 10:00 and 11:00 p.m. that same evening as it returned to the farm.[175]

Henrietta, who had also heard Bailey's wagon late that evening, created her own sensation in the courtroom. A *Boston Post* reporter wrote, "She is a beautiful girl, tall, slight, dark, with large, expressive eyes. She was dressed in a quiet, yet most becoming, manner; in splendid taste. She wore a large black 'picture' hat, a velvet waist and dark skirt. A narrow band of white lace around her shapely throat and a slight, long silver chain were the touches of color in the lovely picture she presented, save for the dark red flush in her cheeks." Attorney General Knowlton later said to one of the court artists, "Young man, make a good picture of Miss Hawkes. I have never seen a more beautiful girl on the witness stand."[176]

By March 22, Best began to show signs of being dejected. His nonchalant air, his firm bearing, his apparent indifference had changed. He twitched nervously in his seat several times and cast nervous glances at the witnesses. While he still professed to reporters a belief that he would be acquitted, his face belied that thought.[177] His depressed mood was not helped by the weather. Dull rain pattered on the windowpanes, and the sky outside was leaden. The gloom of the courtroom was so pronounced that the electric lights were turned on, their yellow light strange and ominous against the gray outside.

When Winnie Rowe was called to testify, the smile that had previously played across Best's face was gone. The strong young farm boy, dressed in a blue serge suit with a low collar and black necktie, told, in his countrified style, about the day that Best had shot within an inch of a target, even though he was partially under the influence of liquor. Best became pale as Rowe recalled that "Best said to me, 'I would give Bailey the privilege of shooting me if he can beat me, and if I beat him, I would want the right to shoot him.'"

At about 5:00 p.m., the reporters began to gather their notes to adjourn, when Knowlton stood and said, "There is one witness that it is important we should put on to-night; I can't tell the reason why, but I would like to have the court trust me in the matter." The reporters settled back with a sigh. John Best put a leg over the arm of his chair and clasped his hands in his lap.

"William H. Stiles," called out District Attorney Peters. Best's brother-in-law took the stand, and Peters asked him what had happened the day before the trial began. Stiles's voice faltered as he replied that he had talked with Best in the Salem jail. He said that Best had given him "a plan of the place, two plans; asked me to get this property and do away with the watch."

"Did he tell you what he wanted you to do away with the watch for?"

"He didn't want it found. He said if the watch was found he was lost. He wanted me to take the watch and 'fling it away as far as I could' was the words used, I believe. Best never told me about Bailey's watch, but told me about a watch. It was in the cellar of the barn in the corner nearest the house."

The courtroom fell silent, and everyone listened intently to the exchange.

"Have you got the plan of the cellar here?"

"No," replied a somber Stiles. "It's in ashes."

"Who burned it?"

"I did."

Best was leaning forward, one hand gripping the arm of his chair.

Stiles continued, "There was a black mark showing the place where the watch was. It was on the first sill in the corner nearest the house."[178]

At that point, state officers Neal and Hammond hurried in their carriage to Breakheart Hill farm, changing their tired horses on the way. State officer

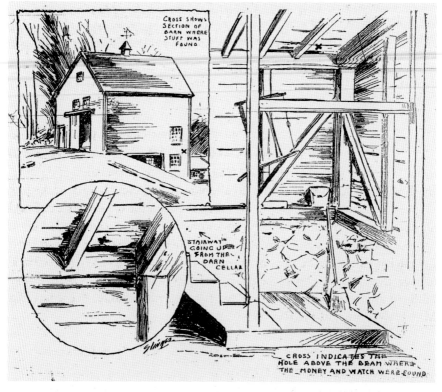

Location of George Bailey's gold watch and money (*X at upper right*), which Best's brother-in-law, William Stiles, revealed in his bombshell trial testimony on March 22, 1901. Drawn by Dwight Sturges. From the *Boston Globe*, March 23, 1901. *Boston Public Library.*

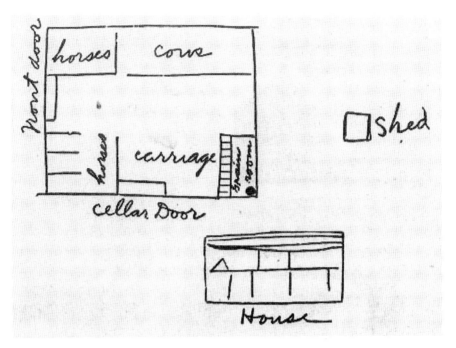

Plan given to William Stiles by John Best. Drawn by Stiles from memory and published by the *Boston Post* on March 25, 1901. Black dot in lower right corner of barn shows where Bailey's gold watch and money were found. *Boston Public Library.*

Harry Proctor and Saugus police chief Thompson joined them in Saugus, and they proceeded to the farm. Neal walked to the barn's cellar door and found it locked. Caretaker Charles Cole heard their arrival and let them in. By the light of a lantern, Neal used a tool to rip up some boards at the foot of the stairs. Finding nothing, he searched between the upper sills and found an opening. He reached his hand in among the cobwebs and pulled out a narrow package wrapped in newspaper and held with a string. Neal carried the package into the farmhouse and opened the package. Wrapped inside a page from a newspaper, they found seventy-two dollars (two ten-dollar bills, ten fives and two ones), a gold watch and a pocketknife. According to a March 1901 issue of the *Boston Post*:

> And now the question is: "Is John Best 'lost,' as he is alleged to have said he should be if the watch was found?"
>
> A Post *reporter arrived upon the scene just as the party were preparing to leave. "Ain't got a word to say; ain't got a word," said excited Officer Neal. "But have you found it?" queried the reporter. "What I've found I*

Watch and money found by Officer Neal near the basement stairs of the Breakheart Hill barn. Susie Young identified these as having belonged to Bailey. *Boston Public Library.*

shall communicate to the district attorney." And away the officers rushed. Mr. Neal was bound for Haverhill. Mr. Charles Cole would not say anything further than: "I would not like to be in John Best's shoes. He is a dead man now."[179]

Meanwhile, a *Boston Globe* reporter stopped by the Stiles home in Lynn to speak with the man who had created such a sensation. William and Nettie Stiles and their ten-year-old son, Earle, were seated in the living room when the reporter entered.

Stiles appeared exceedingly nervous as he spoke with the reporter, telling him:

I did not want to go on the stand, but when once there and after swearing to tell the truth, I could not do otherwise what I did. I was brought up to respect an oath and I am a law-abiding citizen. All I have in this world is honor, and when the lawyers asked me the questions that there was but one answer to: I told the truth. On the stand I felt that all my friends would condemn me, that I would be despised and hated by the world at large, but it was a question of either that or lying deliberately, and I would not do the latter.

Nettie joined the conversation and said she had told her husband to tell the whole truth when he took an oath to do so. However, she firmly believed in her brother's innocence. "I know he is not guilty. He drank at times and was irresponsible when in that condition, but John never murdered Bailey. It is horrible to think he is on trial for his life on this charge when he is innocent."[180]

Susie began her testimony on the afternoon of March 23, 1901. Huge crowds, composed mostly of women, gathered outside of the courthouse in hopes of getting a seat. They had come to see and hear Susie, and even Best was forgotten in their focused interest in the "Woman in the Case."

Two days later, on the second day of her testimony, Susie entered the courthouse early, pale and bespectacled. From a window, she looked out onto the street at the dense crowd and the large number of Salem police. That day, they did not allow a single man to enter the courtroom until some one hundred women had entered.

When the court session began, Susie picked up her story where she had left off. She told District Attorney Peters about how she had met Best, his duties on the farm, the circumstances of her departure, how she had heard about Bailey's disappearance and her correspondence with Best. She described the inside of the farmhouse, the sleeping arrangements and the relationship between the two men. She told about how she often accompanied Bailey on his runs to Deary's dairy farm and what she thought Best did while they were gone.

Peters was particularly interested in the knife with a five- to six-inch blade that Best carried. "When did you first see him have that knife?"

"He drew it out in the kitchen and flourished it around. He said that no one would dare run up against him while he had that knife."

"When did you last see the knife?"

"About two weeks before I came away. He was using it skinning a woodchuck."

Peters asked Susie about Bailey's gold watch.

"He carried it in a watch pocket in his pants and fastened the horse-hair chain to his suspenders."

Peters handed her the gold watch found in the barn on March 22, and she identified it as Bailey's. Peters took an old, torn, weather-stained overcoat and laid it on the rail of the witness box.

"Do you know that coat?"

"I do," Susie said, her voice faltering.

"Whose coat was it?"

"It was George Bailey's coat," she whispered.

Hundreds of eyes fixed on her as she broke her usually remarkable composure and sobbed into her handkerchief. Susie's testimony confirmed the facts and circumstances presented by the prosecution but yielded little new information.[181]

On March 26, Best testified on his own behalf. That morning, the courtroom was lit by electric lights that shone yellow in the gloom as rain beat down on the windows. From the wall above the judge's bench, a portrait of Lemuel Shaw, former chief justice of the Supreme Judicial Court of Massachusetts, looked down with calm eyes as hundreds witnessed Best raise his hand and swear to tell the truth.

Best faced judges, jury, lawyers and spectators with perfect calmness. There was not a tremor in his voice, no hesitancy except an effort to remember and not a trace of fear. He told the full courtroom the story of his life. It was a simple tale, a brief synopsis of an uneventful life, a life of drudgery as farmhand, factory hand and driver of a grocery wagon. Up to the fatal night of October 8, 1900, his life story contained no romance and no hint that it would enter this tragic phase. He claimed that on the night that the murder allegedly took place, he had been slightly drunk and could not recall all that had happened.

Best told the court about finding seventy-four dollars in a candy box and the gold watch in a bureau drawer on the Sunday after Bailey's disappearance. He wrapped these things in a newspaper and hid the package in the barn cellar. He admitted to drawing up plans of the hiding place and giving these to Stiles, as well as asking him to "do away with" the watch. But Best said that it was Stiles who suggested throwing the watch into the sea. Although he admitted that he should not have taken the money and watch—despite what Bailey owed him—he denied the prosecution's claim that he had taken the watch from Bailey's dead body.

"Did you use the words, 'I am lost'?" asked Attorney Sisk.

"I did not."

"Were you afraid that Bailey would return and kill you?"

At this, Best laughed outright, and his mirth seemed genuine. The crowded courtroom grew still, and the spectators leaned forward eagerly. Best faced a strong man—Attorney General Knowlton—in opposition to him. The moment was dramatic, impressive, but Best did not fear Knowlton. He was ready to face him, an answer at hand, or, if he was not quite ready, he requested that the question be repeated. "I have a clear conscience," he declared, emphatically.[182]

The next day, Best's lawyers presented their defense. Over the course of two hours, they claimed that the prosecution had not established that the rifle shots that killed George Bailey were fired on the night of October 8 or that the fatal bullets were discharged from the Winchester rifle found at the farm. However, they said nothing to disprove previous evidence presented

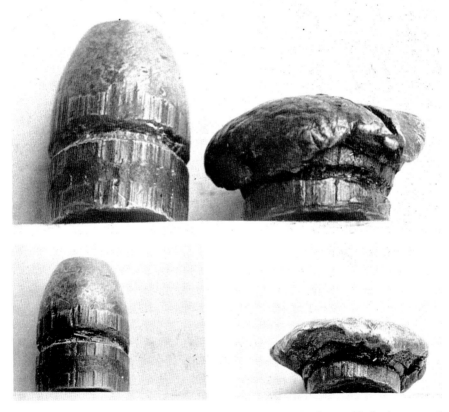

Court exhibits showing the two bullets taken from Bailey's body (flattened bullets) compared to bullets pushed through the .38-caliber Winchester rifle kept at Breakheart Hill farm. Grooves on both sets of bullets matched. Photographs by Waldemar Thode. *Social Law Library, Boston.*

by gun experts. The defense lawyers also denied the prosecution's claim that Best had driven a democrat wagon from Breakheart Hill farm to Floating Bridge Pond, asserting instead that he had been asleep after a night of drinking. During his closing argument for the defense, Sisk exclaimed, "See him, like a madman, five parts of a human body in a wagon, thundering along a brilliantly illuminated, traveled highway, swing into Lake St, on the jump down and on to the bridge, to throw overboard those ghastly bundles! Do you believe it, gentlemen of the jury, do you believe it? Absurd!"[183]

On the morning of the last day of the trial, March 28, 1901, more than two hundred people stood outside the court hoping to gain entry to hear the verdict. When William Stiles and his son, Earle, arrived, they were greeted with cries of "Judas." Since Stiles had testified on March 22, he had been taunted by many area residents. To make matters worse, children, imitating their elders, had begun to bully his young son, and his teachers were unable to prevent it.

When the court doors opened, the police managed, with difficulty, to maintain something like order. Best arrived from the Salem jail and passed through two lines of spectators before entering the court. Just before the jury entered, attorneys Sisk and Clark went up and shook hands with Best and had a whispered conversation, during which Best showed no sign of surprise or fear.[184]

The Verdict

At about 5:00 p.m. on March 28, the jurymen left the courtroom to deliberate. Martha Roberts, the only woman lawyer present, spoke to Best. Smiling, he confidently told her that he was sure he was "all right."[185] The courtroom slowly emptied of spectators, but newspaper reporters remained in the building, not wishing to miss any developments. The justices went to the Salem Club for supper, while the attorney general and the district attorney went to their respective homes in Boston and Haverhill. Meanwhile, a small crowd gathered outside on Federal Street and waited for the jury to return.

At 11:00 p.m., the deathlike stillness of the courtroom was broken by the heavy tread of the defendant as he passed through the doorway in handcuffs, escorted by deputy sheriffs Bishop and Crowley. Best proceeded to his cage and remained standing while the irons were removed from his wrists. He took off his overcoat and laid it on the cage rail and dropped into his seat, his hands twitching while his face assumed a ghostly pallor.

The jury entered the room. Not a whisper was heard as Justices Sherman and Fox took their places at the bench. The court clerk called Best to rise. As he rose, he fell forward slightly toward the front rail of the cage.[186]

"Gentlemen of the jury, have you agreed upon a verdict?" the clerk asked.

"We have," answered the twelve men in unison.

"Who shall speak for you?"

"The foreman," the jury replied.

"John C. Best, hold up your right hand. Mr. Foreman, look upon the prisoner; prisoner, look upon the foreman. What say you, Mr. Foreman? Is John C. Best, the prisoner at the bar, guilty or not guilty?"

"Guilty of murder in the first degree."

"Gentlemen of the jury, hearken to your verdict as the court have recorded it. You, upon your oath, do say that John C. Best is guilty of murder in the first degree? So say you, Mr. Foreman, so say you all?"

"We do."[187]

When the foreman announced the guilty verdict, Best appeared dazed for a few seconds and then rallied somewhat. He trembled and turned white. Attorney Sisk walked over to the cage and whispered words of consolation. As he did this, tears welled up in his eyes, showing more emotion than the man just condemned to death. Finally, Judge Sherman said, "I wish to thank you, gentlemen of the jury, for your faithful service on this case. The prisoner has had a fair trial and has been defended by able counsel. I think we must be satisfied that this is the proper verdict."[188]

From the start of their deliberations, the jury had agreed that Best was guilty. Without any witnesses to the crime, it had become clear during the trial that Best had the means, motive and opportunity to commit the crime. In fact, he had three motives. First, he was infatuated with Susie, and if she believed that Bailey had run away and deserted her, Best seemed to think that Susie would become his wife or mistress. Second, Best believed that Bailey had about $500, which partly belonged to him. He was, however, mistaken about the amount, which was considerably less. Third, he believed that the owners of the farm would make him caretaker if he could convince them that Bailey had run away.

Although he had motives to commit the crime, Best might not have been convicted if Bailey's body had not been found. Without a body, Best's attorneys could have argued that Bailey had fled to an unknown location to avoid prosecution for abandoning his family in Maine. The murderer had

John C. Best hears the jury's verdict: "Guilty of Murder in the First Degree." Drawn by court artist Charles Lawrence. From the *Lynn Daily Evening Item*, March 29, 1901. *Lynn Public Library.*

made the mistake of not putting a heavy enough stone in the burlap bag that held Bailey's torso. The twenty-eight-pound stone was heavy enough to sink the bag but not heavy enough to stop it from floating to the surface as it filled with gases from decomposition. But for this crucial detail, Best would likely have remained a free man.

Although the jury had unanimously decided that Best was guilty, they had struggled to decide whether he was guilty in the first or second degree.

Murder in the first degree meant that the murder was deliberate and premeditated, punishable by death. Murder in the second degree meant life in prison. After five hours of deliberation and several rounds of voting, all jurors settled on murder in the first degree.

The verdict did not stop attorney Sisk from fighting for Best's life. With an air of great seriousness, he said, "If your honor please, I wish to state that it is our intention to file a motion to set aside this decree. How much time can we have to file exceptions?"

"Any time you want," Judge Sherman replied.

"A month?"

"Yes."[189]

The news that Best had been convicted of murder spread like wildfire. Most had thought that, similar to the 1893 Lizzie Borden case, guilty or not, circumstantial evidence would not be enough to condemn Best to the electric chair. Many believed that Best would not have been convicted if not for William Stiles revealing the evidence of the money and watch.

A *Boston Globe* reporter was the first person to convey the verdict to Stiles, Susie Young and Charles Bailey, brother of the murdered man. "My God, this is a terrible blow," said Stiles when the reporter notified him of the verdict at his home just before midnight. With his hands clasped to his head, he moaned aloud and deplored the conviction. "This blow will probably kill my wife. She has been sick all day, and her nerves are all gone. She is lying upstairs, and absolutely refuses to rest until she has heard the verdict. It is not improbable another life will be sacrificed in this trouble."

As the reporter took his leave, Stiles said, "My conscience is clear. I did all I could for John and never said a word to anybody regarding what Best told me about the watch and money until I was put on the stand. I took an oath to tell the truth and I did it. My God I am sorry for this."

Susie Young and Charles Bailey took the news of the verdict entirely differently from Stiles. Susie was in a room at the Winthrop House in Lynn when the reporter knocked loudly on the door. When told of the verdict, she said, "I am glad. He was guilty and deserves to be punished. It may seem to be a terrible thing to say, but I believe I could watch him when he goes to the electric chair." Susie then said that she would leave for her home in Wiscasset the following afternoon.

Charles, who was staying in a room near Susie's, heard the news from the reporter with a smile. "He is guilty of killing my brother, and I am certainly pleased that he will have to suffer for it."[190]

APPEALS AND LAST DAYS

O n Saturday afternoon, March 30, 1901, two days after the trial ended, Attorney Sisk filed a motion with the clerk of courts in Salem to set aside the verdict and allow a new trial. Best's defense lawyers claimed that the verdict was "against the evidence....Against the weight of the evidence.... Against the law." They also claimed that one of the jurors, James Trask, was "disqualified to serve...owing to the fact that he was deaf."[191]

Between January and May 1902, the Massachusetts Supreme Court heard their arguments and denied all motions and overruled all exceptions. In early June, having exhausted all appeals to the higher courts, Sisk visited Best at the Salem jail and said, "John, I have rather bad news for you."

"Turned down again?"

"Yes."

"I am disappointed. I had considerable hope of that. I heard every word of evidence, and I don't see how they could find that juror was competent to sit on my case."

Sisk made a final appeal to Governor Winthrop Crane to commute Best's sentence to life imprisonment, but the verdict was upheld.[192]

Best's parents followed the news with horror from their home in Sackville, New Brunswick, and wrote to Reverend Isaac Mellish, a Methodist minister in Salem:

> *Dear Sir—Will you please go and see our dear son John, now under sentence of death in Salem jail as often as you can until the sentence is*

carried out. We are so far away that it will be a great comfort to us to know that some one thinks of him and is interested in him, and we know that John would like to have you visit him. Please accept our heartfelt thanks for your kindness and sympathy in our sore trouble.

Yours, very truly,

Thomas Best

Zilpha Best

West Sackville, New Brunswick[193]

At 9:20 a.m. on June 13, 1902, deputy sheriffs Crowley and Bishop brought Best to the Salem Superior Court. A large crowd milled about the entrance, including many women. Best was neatly dressed and cleanly shaven, appearing quite bright as he entered the courthouse, nodded to Reverend Mellish and talked with his counsels, Sisk and Clark. A deathlike stillness pervaded the room before the court officials came in.

Justice Edgar Sherman took his seat, and the crier made the usual proclamation. District Attorney Peters addressed the court, "Best has had a fair trial and was ably defended. I now move that sentence be passed."

"What the district attorney has said is true," Sherman said. "I wish to say that the court sympathizes with you; I now proceed with that sentence. It is considered by the court that you be put to death by the passage of a current of electricity through your body during the week commencing on Sunday, September 7, in his infinite goodness, have mercy on your soul." Best received his sentence without evidence of emotion and, at once, took his seat. The court adjourned.

During July, Reverend Mellish met frequently with Best at the Salem jail. On one occasion, he told reporters that Best was in "good spirits and still asserts that he is innocent of the crime of which he has been convicted."[194]

On August 28, Best was transferred from the Salem jail to Charlestown State Prison. Two days later, his father, Thomas, and two sisters, Mabel and Maud, traveled to Boston to visit him on murderers' row in a part of the prison known as Fort Russell. One sister told a reporter, "Our parents believe his statements as to his innocence, and so do those at his old home in Middle Sackville, New Brunswick, who knew him as a boy and never thought of such an ending to his life."[195] The following day, Thomas returned to Sackville.[196]

On September 7, Best sat composed and quiet in his cell. By law, the execution was to take place between midnight and sunrise of a day during the week of September 7. The warden had the duty of setting the exact date, but he could only disclose it to the legal witnesses.[197]

The prison warden was to come for the condemned man at midnight on September 8. That day, the *Boston Post* reported that "Best is nervous as the ordeal draws near.…Yesterday he spent in preparing a last statement which he will give to the world. It is intimated that the long-looked-for confession is at hand. He continually assails his brother-in-law, William H. Stiles of Lynn, whose testimony alone Best believes convicted him."[198]

Reverend Mellish related his last conversation with Best to a *Boston Traveler* reporter: "John, you're getting nearer to your end. Now while I realize these feelings are our honest convictions, I beg you not to carry this feeling that injustice has been done to you any further. The time has come, less than an hour, and I want you to go out of the world at peace with yourself, your God and the world."

"I'll tell you, Mr. Mellish. I am at peace with myself and my God, but I can't say so of the world."

"How's that, John?"

"Do you think the Lord expects me to forgive the man who put me here? It's an awful hard thing to do. Do you think that the Lord requires it of me?"

"Yes," Mellish said. "I know so."

The reverend then quoted passages from the scripture that led Best to say, "Mr. Mellish, I've been wronged, but I forgive them from the bottom of my heart."

On the evening of September 8, Best was escorted out of his cell and shook hands with the prison officers. Reverend Mellish then took Best by the hand and said, "John, what's the last word?"

"I'm an innocent man, and I hope we'll meet again," Best replied clearly and firmly.[199]

At midnight, John Best walked to the electric chair unassisted and "sat down composedly as one would wait for a train at a station, assisted the guards even in the operations of confining his hands and legs, and awaited the shock of the current in perfect composure." He had no word to say or confession to make and was pronounced dead at 12:27 a.m., the fourth man in Massachusetts to be electrocuted.

The state refused his family's request to return his body to New Brunswick. Instead, prison officials transported Best's remains in a horse-drawn wagon to Massachusetts Reformatory Cemetery in Concord and marked his grave with a simple white concrete marker stamped "MSP 105."

On his last day alive, Best gave a letter to Reverend Mellish to deliver to his parents. Eleven days later, a copy was published in the *Evening Times* of Pawtucket, Rhode Island. In it, Best maintained his innocence, saying,

The Concord Reformatory Cemetery in Concord, Massachusetts. John Best's grave is designated "Massachusetts State Police (MSP) No. 105." Many prisoners who died or were executed at the Charlestown State Prison are buried here. *Photograph by Alison C. Simcox.*

"One thing I would like to impress on the mind of you, my father and mother, is that it is not God's will that I lose this life that he has given me, but through the vengeance and ignorance of men....I am not afraid to die, but I would like to live. I don't compare myself to Christ, our Savior, but my condemnation is on the same line as His, and I will meet death as calmly as he did. If these lines, my dear father and mother, will give you any comfort, I am well paid for writing them."[200]

EPILOGUE

Susie Young

After the trial, Susie returned to Wiscasset, Maine, relieved to be out of the media spotlight and anxious to begin an ordinary life. In October 1905, she married engineer Frank Farnsworth and changed her name to Susanna. By 1910, they had moved to Fitchburg, Massachusetts, where Farnsworth worked as a garage chauffeur. Susie's young son, Franklin, however, stayed behind in Maine to work for farmers George and Kezir Pinkham. By 1918, Frank and Susie were no longer together. Two years later, she was living in a rooming house in Portland, Maine, under the name Anna May Farnsworth.

Grave of Susie Young and her husband, Oren Hutchins, at Mount Feake Cemetery in Waltham, Massachusetts. *Photograph by Douglas L. Heath.*

In 1924, she married Oren Hutchins, ten years her junior. By 1930, they had moved to Waltham, Massachusetts, where Hutchins worked as a machinist at the Waltham Watch Company. He died in April 1967, and Susie died seven months later at age ninety.

Franklin Paul Bailey

During Best's trial, three-year-old Franklin (George Bailey's ninth child) stayed with Susie's parents in Wiscasset. He attended school there through the eighth grade before going to live and work with farmers George and Kezir Pinkham in Newcastle, Maine. In 1918, he enlisted in the military but, for unknown reasons, did not serve. Instead, he worked at a sawmill in Bath, Maine. Two years later, he was working as an erector in the Bath shipyards and living in a boardinghouse. By 1930, Franklin owned a pumpkin farm in Mount Vernon, Maine, and in 1932, he married Stella Coffin Wing, more than twenty years his senior. She died in 1959, and he died in 1968. They had no children, and no photos of Franklin are available.

Abbie (Hilton) Bailey

When Bailey fled Maine with Susie Young in 1897, he left his wife, Abbie, and their five living children destitute. Abbie became a ward of Wiscasset, while their daughters, Sadie, Ethel and Reta, went to live at two farms in Whitefield. Their son Charles was sent to the State Reform School for Boys in South Portland. George Edward Jr. lived with George Cookson, a Whitefield blacksmith, and his wife, Fannie. A family photograph including George Edward Jr., Sadie and other family members was taken in 1924.

Bailey family about 1924. (*Left to right*): unknown man; George Bailey Jr.; probably Abbie Hilton Bailey Wing; Sadie Bailey with her daughter, Louise Ware; Clara Bailey, second wife of George Bailey Jr.; and Harold Pitcher, third husband of Sadie. *Mary Lou Bailey.*

Gravesite of twenty-three-year-old Charles Bailey, George and Abbie's son, at Whitefield Cemetery, Maine. In foreground, from left to right, are markers for Charles's mother, Abbie (George's second wife), and her second husband, Harry Wing; Charles; Charles's father, George Bailey ("father"); and George's first wife, Mary McNutt ("wife"). *Photograph by Alison C. Simcox.*

In 1902, Abbie married Harry Wing, a plumber from Brunswick, Maine, and Charles returned from reform school to live with them. Wing worked as a teamster for a truck team, a plumber and an assistant undertaker at a funeral home. By 1936, Abbie was a widow living in Bath. Harry and Abbie are buried at the Whitefield (Maine) Cemetery in the same plot as George Bailey; George and Abbie's son, Charles; and Bailey's first wife, Mary (McNutt) Bailey. This strange gravesite was probably laid out and paid for by George Bailey's mother after the death of her grandson Charles in 1911.

William and Nettie Stiles

Shortly after John Best's March 1901 trial, the Stiles family returned to Nova Scotia, probably to escape the persecution William suffered during and after the trial, when he was accused of betraying his brother-in-law, and the bullying that their son, Earle, was subjected to at school. They moved to Brookvale, near John Best's hometown of Sackville, New Brunswick. William became a farmer, and in 1910, they had another child, Clara. William died in 1941, and Nettie died in 1944.

State Officer George Neal

In 1905, George Neal was appointed Massachusetts fire marshal, a post he held for twenty-five years. During that time, he helped restrict the sale of dynamite in Massachusetts and started a campaign for a "Safe and Sane Fourth of July." In 1929, Neal died in Lynn of pneumonia at age eighty-seven. Governor Allen attended his funeral, which included a retinue of mounted state officers.

Attorney General Hosea Knowlton

Before serving as chief prosecutor in John Best's trial, Hosea Knowlton had gained fame in this same role in the notorious 1893 Lizzie Borden trial. Despite Knowlton's able handling of the Borden case, the evidence was circumstantial (as it was in Best's trial), and the jury determined that the prosecution had failed to prove guilt beyond a reasonable doubt. Knowlton became Massachusetts attorney general in 1894, replacing Arthur Pillsbury, and was reelected four times. Despite being a prosecutor for capital crimes, he was an advocate for abolishing capital punishment in New England. He wrote, "I have no conscientious scruples against it, but I believe that the statute for the death penalty is not in accord with our civilization, nor is it wise policy." In 1902, Knowlton died in Marion, Massachusetts, following a stroke.

Attorney James Sisk

Despite his unsuccessful defense of John Best, Sisk was a highly successful lawyer. In 1915, he was appointed an associate justice of the Massachusetts Superior Court, a post he held for twenty-two years. In 1925, he sentenced

Charles Ponzi (of Ponzi scheme fame), whom he called "a common and notorious thief," to seven to nine years in Charlestown State Prison, and in 1927, he denied a stay of execution for Sacco and Vanzetti. Sisk died in Lynn in 1938.

Winfield "Winnie" Rowe

In July 1904, Rowe began work as a trolley motorman on the Boston & Northern Railway. After just two months on the job, he replaced the regular motorman, Henry Watson, on an evening run from Boston's Scollay Square to Melrose. At about 8:00 p.m. on September 21, while crossing Wyoming Avenue on Main Street in Melrose with thirty-two passengers, the trolley wheels struck a box containing fifty pounds of dynamite. The box had fallen from a wagon driven by twenty-five-year-old Roy Fenton. When Fenton turned back to retrieve it, there was a terrific explosion, which broke windows and tossed bodies hundreds of feet from the mangled trolley. Rowe's body was found nearly three hundred feet from the blast. Four other people were killed instantly, and another four died in hospital. Later, Rowe was found to not be responsible for the disaster because nearby streetlamps were not working.

Breakheart Hill Farm

Shortly after John Best's trial, Charles Cole, who had replaced George Bailey as caretaker, left Breakheart Hill farm. The three Lynn businessmen who owned the property hired a local milkman and former railroad laborer, George Parker, to replace Cole. George and Lucinda Parker moved to the farm with their five children, and in June 1901, a sixth child was born there. George died in 1923, but his family lived on the farm for another two years. After 1925, there appears to have been no more caretakers.

In 1934, executors for Benjamin Johnson and Micajah Clough sold the entire six-hundred-acre Breakheart property to the Metropolitan District Commission (MDC), which leased it to the federal government. In June 1935, the farm's apple orchard and hayfield were destroyed and replaced by Civilian Conservation Corps (CCC) barracks for two hundred young men.

The farmhouse became an administration building, and the barn was used to store vehicles and equipment. After World War II, the federal government returned the property to the state. In 1946, the MDC razed the CCC barracks, and in 1973, it demolished the barn and farmhouse due to unsafe conditions, mostly from termite damage. The basements of both buildings were filled in and the site landscaped. In 1987, MDC chief archaeologist Thomas Mahlstedt convinced state officials to save the historic area from becoming a parking lot.

NOTES

Chapter 1

1. "History," Town of Alna, Maine, https://www.alna.maine.gov.
2. *Lynn Daily Evening Item*, October 20, 1900.
3. "Saugus, MA (1873)," Celebrate Boston, Boston Culture, http://www.celebrateboston.com.
4. *Wakefield Daily Item*, October 19, 1900.
5. William H Mulligan Jr., "The Shoemakers of Lynn, Massachusetts, 1850–1880: The Family during the Transition from Hand to Machine Labor" (PhD diss., Clark University, 1982), https://eh.net; Paul G. Faler, *Mechanics and Manufacturers in the Early Industrial Revolution, Lynn, Massachusetts 1780–1860* (Albany: State University of New York Press, 1981), 267.
6. *Lynn Directory for 1882* (Boston: Sampson, Murdock & Co., 1882).
7. Alonzo Lewis and James Newhall, *History of Lynn, Essex County, Massachusetts, Including Lynnfield, Saugus, Swampscott, and Nahant* (Lynn, MA: George C. Herbert, 1865), 330.
8. *Lynn Daily Evening Item*, October 20, 1900; *Massachusetts Vital Records, 1840–1911* (Boston: New England Historic Genealogical Society).
9. U.S. City Directories, 1822–1995, 2011, Ancestry.com.
10. Lewis and Newhall, *History of Lynn*, 278.
11. Lynn, Massachusetts Population History, 1840–2017, https://www.biggestuscities.com.
12. *Lynn Directory, 1869–1873* (Boston: Sampson, Davenport & Co.).

13. "Intake Record: McNutt, Charles H," Tewksbury Almshouse Intake Records [1854–1884], https://tewksburyalms.omeka.net.

14. Massachusetts Death Records, 1841–1915, Sarah McNutt, City of Lynn, 1873.

15. "Cholera in the 19th Century," Lamb Collection, https://sites.scran.ac.uk.

16. Census records for Massachusetts, 1850–80, https://www.archives.gov. Records of Mary and Ruth McNutt at Lynn Almshouse are on Roll 33.

17. Lewis and Newhall, *History of Lynn*, 276; VCU Libraries Social Welfare History Project, includes articles about almshouses; Massachusetts Marriage Records, 1840–1915, Ancestry.com; First [-seventh] Annual Report of the State Board of Health, Lunacy and Charity [1879–1885], Boston, MA, 1880–86.

18. *Boston Globe*, October 20, 1900; *Lynn Daily Evening Item*, October 20, 1900.

19. *Chelsea, Revere and Winthrop Directory for the Year 1889*, no. 22 (Chelsea, MA: Charles L. Sale), 185.

20. *Lynn Daily Evening Item*, October 26, 1900.

21. *Boston Globe*, October 20, 1900.

22. Ibid.

23. *Boston Daily Advertiser*, October 23, 1900.

24. *Boston Globe*, October 23, 1900.

25. Ibid., October 20, 1900.

26. "Maine Industrial School for Girls," Maine Memory Network, Historic Hallowell, http://historichallowell.mainememory.net.

27. "Wiscasset Jail and Museum," Wikipedia; "1812 Jail," Town of Wiscasset, Maine, http://wiscasset.org.

28. *Boston Globe*, October 23, 1900.

29. Lincoln County Historical Association Jail Calendar (1879–1893), Wiscasset Jail and Museum, Wiscasset, Maine.

30. Ibid.

31. Maine Birth Records, 1715–1922, Augusta, Maine, Maine State Archives.

32. *Boston Globe*, October 23, 1900.

33. *Lynn Daily Evening Item*, October 20, 1900.

34. *Boston Globe*, October 23, 1900.

35. Ibid., October 20, 1900.

36. *Lynn Daily Evening Item*, October 20, 1900.

37. *Boston Globe*, October 20, 1900.

Chapter 2

38. 1881 Census of Canada, 2009, Ancestry.com.
39. *Boston Post*, October 22, 1900.
40. *Lynn Directory for 1886* (Boston: Sampson, Murdock & Co).
41. The Official Report of the Trial of John C. Best, Superior Court of Massachusetts, 1903, 662–63 (hereafter Trial Report).
42. Ibid., 663.
43. *Lynn Directory for 1892* (Boston: Sampson, Murdock & Co), 565; *Boston Globe*, October 24, 1900.
44. *Lynn Daily Evening Item*, October 19, 22, 1900; Trial Report, 667.
45. *Lynn Daily Evening Item*, October 20, 1900.
46. *Boston Globe*, October 19, 1900.
47. Trial Report, 663–64.
48. *Boston Globe*, June 14, 1899; *Lynn Daily Evening Item*, June 19, 1899; Trial Report, 664; Howard Zinn, "The Lynn Shoe Strike, 1860," https://libcom.org; Jeffrey Helgeson, *American Labor and Working-Class History, 1900–1945* (Oxford, UK: Oxford University Press, 2016).
49. Trial Report, 664.

Chapter 3

50. Twelfth Census of the United States, 1900, National Archives and Records Administration, T623, 1854 rolls.
51. Alison C. Simcox and Douglas L. Heath, *Breakheart Reservation* (Charlestown, SC: Arcadia Publishing, 2013).
52. Trial Report, 410.
53. Southern Essex District Registry of Deeds, Salem, MA.
54. Trial Report, 411.
55. Marcia Wiswell Lindberg, *Daniel and Joseph Hitchings of Lynn, Continued* (Salem, MA: Essex Genealogist, 1992); U.S. and Canada, Passenger and Immigration Lists Index, 1500s–1900s, 2010, Ancestry.com.
56. Trial Report, 492.
57. Ibid., 508.
58. Ibid., 100.
59. *Boston Herald*, October 27, 1900.
60. *Lynn Daily Evening Item*, October 20, 1900.
61. *Boston Herald*, October 27, 1900

62. *Boston Globe*, October 22, 1900.

63. *Boston Daily Advertiser*, October 22, 1900.

64. *Boston Post*, October 22, 1900.

65. *Lynn Daily Evening Item*, October 27, 1900.

66. Trial Report, 664.

67. Ibid., 665.

68. Ibid., 664–65.

69. Ibid., 392.

70. Ibid., 666; *Boston Daily Advertiser*, October 25, 1900.

71. Trial Report, 666.

72. Ibid., 667.

73. Ibid., 668.

74. *Boston Herald*, October 23, 1900.

75. *Boston Globe*, October 22, 1900.

76. Trial Report, 378.

77. Ibid., 378–79, 384.

78. Ibid., 372–74.

79. *Boston Evening Record*, October 19, 1900.

80. Trial Report, 502.

81. *Boston Journal*, October 19, 1900.

82. *Boston Globe*, October 22, 1900.

83. Trial Report, 410.

84. Ibid., 257.

85. Ibid., 220.

86. Ibid., 722.

87. Ibid., 98–99, 306.

88. Ibid., 73, 532, 669.

89. Ibid., 193.

90. Ibid., 194.

Chapter 4

91. Trial Report, 353–56.

92. Ibid., 241.

93. Ibid., 222–24.

94. Ibid., 225–26.

95. *Lynn Daily Evening Item*, October 20, 1900; Trial Report, 258–61.

96. Trial Report, 196.

97. Ibid., 258–62.
98. Ibid., 357.
99. Ibid., 241.
100. Ibid., 287–97; *Boston Globe*, October 20, 1900.
101. Trial Report, 358.
102. Trial Report, 295; "Clay Tobacco Pipe—TD Style," Odysseys Virtual Museum, http://www.odysseysvirtualmuseum.com.
103. Trial Report, 296–97; *Boston Globe*, October 21, 1900.
104. Trial Report, 263–65.
105. Ibid., 404–6.
106. Ibid., 359, 367.
107. *Boston Globe*, October 28, 1900; *Beverly Evening Times*, October 29, 1900.
108. Trial Report, 501–3.
109. Ibid., 406–7.
110. Ibid., 498; *Boston Evening Reporter*, October 19, 1900.
111. Trial Report, 521.
112. Ibid., 435–36, 439.
113. Ibid., 408–9.

Chapter 5

114. *Lynn Daily Evening Item*, October 17, 1900. The bridge over Floating Bridge (or Glenmere) Pond was built in the early 1800s on pontoons because the pond bottom was too soft to drive piles. Thus, a legend arose that the pond was bottomless.
115. *Boston Morning Journal*, October 18, 1900.
116. Trial Report, 41.
117. Ibid., 40–44.
118. *Lynn Daily Evening Item*, October 17, 1900.
119. Trial Report, 68.
120. *Boston Globe*, October 19, 1900.
121. Trial Report, 436–37; *Boston Globe*, October 20, 1900.
122. *Boston Herald*, October 18, 1900.
123. Henry Fenno, *Our Police: The Official History of the Police Department of the City of Lynn from the First Constable to the Latest Appointee* (Lynn, MA: City of Lynn, 1895).
124. Trial Report, 45–47.
125. Ibid., 61.

Chapter 6

126. Trial Report, 457, 474.
127. Ibid., 613–15.
128. Ibid., 525–29; *Boston Globe*, October 18, 1900; *Boston Herald*, October 18, 1900.
129. *Boston Globe*, October 18, 1900.
130. Trial Report, 530.
131. *Boston Herald*, October 18, 1900.
132. Trial Report, 498.

Chapter 7

133. Fenno, *Our Police*, 206.
134. *Boston Globe*, October 18, 1900.
135. *Lynn Daily Evening Item*, October 18, 1900.
136. *Boston Globe*, October 18, 1900.
137. *Lynn Daily Evening Item*, October 20, 1900.
138. *Boston Daily American*, October 18, 1900.
139. *Boston Herald*, October 19, 1900.
140. *Boston Globe*, October 19, 1900.
141. Ibid.
142. *Boston Evening Reporter*, October 19, 1900; *Boston Globe*, October 19, 1900.
143. *Boston Herald*, October 20, 1900; *Boston Globe*, October 20, 1900.
144. *Boston Globe*, October 20, 1900.
145. *Lynn Daily Evening Item*, October 20, 1900.
146. *Boston Globe*, October 25, 1900.
147. *Boston Daily American*, October 25, 1900; *Boston Globe*, October 25, 1900.
148. *Boston Post*, October 22, 1900.
149. *Boston Globe*, October 23, 1900.
150. Ibid., October 24, 1900.
151. Ibid., October 25, 1900.
152. Ibid.
153. *Boston Post*, October 26, 1900.
154. *Boston Globe*, October 27, 1900.
155. *Boston Post*, October 29, 1900.
156. *Boston Globe*, October 30, 1900.
157. *Lynn Daily Evening Item*, November 2, 1900.

158. *Boston Globe*, November 8, 1900.
159. *Boston Post*, November 9, 1900; *Boston Globe*, November 9, 1900.
160. Ibid., November 10, 1900.
161. *Boston Globe*, November 10, 1900.
162. Ibid., November 10, 1900.
163. *Boston Post*, February 23, 1901

Chapter 8

164. Denise Noe, "A Portrait of Hosea Knowlton, District Attorney for the Prosecution in the Lizzie Borden Trial," *The Hatchet: Journal of Lizzie Borden Studies* 3, no. 1 (February/March 2006).
165. *Salem Evening News*, March 18, 1901.
166. *Boston Globe*, October 18, 1901.
167. Trial Report, 6–11; *Boston Herald*, March 19, 1901.
168. *Salem Evening News*, March 20, 1901; *Boston Globe*, March 20, 1901.
169. *Boston Post*, March 20, 1901.
170. *Boston Globe*, March 20, 1901.
171. *Boston Post*, March 20, 1901.
172. Trial Report, 12–33.
173. *Boston Post*, March 20, 1901.
174. Ibid., March 21, 1901.
175. Ibid.
176. Ibid.
177. Ibid., March 22, 1901.
178. Trial Report, 394; *Boston Post*, March 23, 1901.
179. *Boston Post*, March 23, 1901.
180. *Boston Globe*, March 23, 1901.
181. *Boston Post*, March 26, 1901.
182. Ibid., March 28, 1901.
183. *Boston Globe*, March 28, 1901; Trial Report, 758.
184. *Salem Evening News*, March 28, 1901.
185. Ibid., March 29, 1901.
186. *Boston Globe*, March 29, 1901; *Salem Evening News*, March 29, 1901.
187. Trial Report, 828; *Boston Globe*, March 29, 1901
188. *Boston Globe*, March 29, 1901.
189. Ibid.
190. Ibid.

Chapter 9

191. *Salem Evening News*, March 30, 1901.
192. *Boston Globe*, April 12, June 4, 1902.
193. Ibid., July 13, 1902.
194. Ibid., June 14, 1902.
195. *Boston Post*, August 30, 1902.
196. Ibid., September 1, 1902.
197. *Boston Globe*, September 8, 1902.
198. *Boston Post*, September 8, 1902.
199. *Boston Traveler*, September 9, 1902.
200. Ibid.; *Boston Globe*, September 9, 1902; *Evening Times* (Pawtucket, RI), September 20, 1902.